"Confidence, independence and resilience are among the core dispositions that students not only bring into the classroom but, as this book demonstrates, can be taught. Here's how."

— **John Hattie**, *Professor and Director of the Melbourne Education Research Institute, University of Melbourne, Australia*

"Character education has proved a very tricky issue for schools. It's hard to define and even harder to turn into something of value in the classroom; even the terminology is unhelpful. In this incredibly valuable book Matt Lloyd-Rose manages to provide a clear and readable synthesis of the current state of research and a set of practical recommendations that teachers can use day to day. A must read for anyone working in schools."

— **Sam Freedman**, *Executive Director for Participant Impact and Delivery at TeachFirst, UK*

"Matt is an insightful thinker and he has produced an insightful book. He has been working on character since before it was fashionable and there is much to take from the book for teachers and school leaders."

— **Ed Vainker**, *Principal, Reach Academy Feltham, UK*

"Matt Lloyd-Rose has written a compelling and accessible book about the importance of creating an ambitious, nurturing classroom culture. He provides detailed insight into the strategies taken by a range of teachers determined to build their pupils' positive energy for learning. This book will inspire teachers and give practical advice about how to create a culture of opportunity for every pupil, where learning has no limits."

— **Dame Alison Peacock**, *Chartered College of Teaching, UK*

THE CHARACTER CONUNDRUM

The Character Conundrum is a practical guide for developing confidence, independence and resilience in primary and secondary classrooms. Tackling the hotly-contested question of what role schools can play in developing 'character', the book untangles the big debates in this area and outlines how teachers can support their pupils to develop the skills and mindsets that will help them to thrive academically.

Based on a combination of ground-level investigations and academic research, the book offers a simple, evidence-based approach that can be implemented at every level of school life. The key to this approach is being deliberate and consistent: knowing which mindsets, skills and habits you're trying to develop, and planning the details of your classroom culture, relationships, routines and instruction so that they align and combine to address your aims. When you do this, the author contends, seemingly minor changes to your practice can have a major effect on pupils. The book contains a step-by-step guide to bringing this approach to life in your classroom, including a framework of pupil outcomes, a flowchart of teacher actions, classroom case studies and a wealth of tried-and-tested strategies from primary and secondary schools across the UK.

A lack of confidence, independence and resilience is a major barrier to learning for many pupils and dilutes other efforts that schools make to support them. *The Character Conundrum* argues that teachers can help pupils develop these characteristics in any school context and illustrates how they can do so within and through their day-to-day teaching. Written with passion and clarity, it will be essential reading for primary and secondary teachers, as well as policy makers with an interest in 'character', grit and resilience, and any education professionals committed to giving students greater ownership of their learning and setting them up to succeed.

Matt Lloyd-Rose is a social researcher, NGO leader and writer. Matt worked as a classroom teacher before becoming Associate Director for Knowledge Development at Teach First, UK, where he led a research team investigating how schools can address educational inequality.

THE CHARACTER CONUNDRUM

How to Develop Confidence, Independence and Resilience in the Classroom

Matt Lloyd-Rose

Routledge
Taylor & Francis Group

LONDON AND NEW YORK

First published 2018
by Routledge
2 Park Square, Milton Park, Abingdon, Oxon OX14 4RN

and by Routledge
711 Third Avenue, New York, NY 10017

Routledge is an imprint of the Taylor & Francis Group, an informa business

British Library Cataloguing in Publication Data
A catalogue record for this book is available from the British Library

Library of Congress Cataloging in Publication Data
A catalog record for this book has been requested

ISBN: 978-1-138-73075-5 (hbk)
ISBN: 978-1-138-73076-2 (pbk)
ISBN: 978-1-315-18926-0 (ebk)

Typeset in Caslon and Gill Sans
by Sunrise Setting Ltd., Brixham, UK
Printed and bound by CPI Group (UK) Ltd, Croydon, CR0 4YY

For all of the teachers and pupils who welcomed my team into their classrooms.

CONTENTS

CAST LIST

The research that underpins this book was conducted in schools around the country while I was leading the Knowledge Development team at the charity Teach First. My team and I visited teachers in a wide range of year groups, subjects, and types of school, and in very different local contexts. The examples in this book are drawn from distinctively different classrooms but they have two things in common: the teachers all trained to teach through the Teach First programme; and they are all in schools in economically deprived communities.

The following teachers appear in this guide, referred to throughout by their first name, generally without details of their phase, subject or location. Their details are listed for reference here:

Hayley Brand: Secondary Science, London
Chris Brolly: Secondary English, North West
Patrick Carey: Year 3, West Midlands
Nicky Carney: Secondary MFL, North West
Charlie Maxwell: Year 3, West Midlands
Ally Demicoli: Year 2, London
Becky Donaldson: Secondary Maths, London
James Emanuel: Year 3, London
Lawrence Foley: Secondary English, London
Lowri Goldsmith: Year 4, West Midlands
Rebekah Hawthornthwaite: Secondary English, North West
Lucy Jacobs: Secondary Maths, North West
Stephen Hughes: Year 4, North East
Alice Gordon: Year 6, London
Thomas Young: Secondary English, London
Andreas Michaels: Secondary English, West Midlands
Susannah Meersand: Secondary RE, West Midlands

Kayleigh Meyrick: Secondary MFL, Yorkshire and the Humber
Dan Morrison: Secondary English, London
Sarah Norman: Secondary English, West Midlands
Charlotte Norwood: Secondary MFL, North West
Joe Pardoe: Secondary History, Yorkshire and the Humber
Rebecca Peck: Year 1, East Midlands
Elizabeth Price: Year 1, East Midlands
Nicole Quenault: Reception, South East
Katie Roberts: Secondary Science, West Midlands
Deborah Sloan: Secondary Languages, North East
Jessica Spry-Leverton: Year 4, London
James Storey: Secondary History, Yorkshire and the Humber
Lian Tan: Year 2, Yorkshire and the Humber
Mark Salter: Secondary Maths, London
Sam Waller: Year 2, East Midlands

All pupils, and some teachers, in this guide have been anonymised.

INTRODUCTION

From 2012 to 2015 I led a research team at the charity Teach First investigating teaching in primary and secondary schools in England's poorest communities. We watched lessons and interviewed teachers and pupils, trying to define the things teachers do that have the greatest impact. My first visit was to a secondary English teacher called Dan, who taught at a school in Croydon, and I phoned him the evening before to firm up details. Everything was set for the visit, Dan told me, but he wanted me to know that the Deputy Head would also be observing his Year 11 English lesson.

'Do you still want me to come?' I asked.

'You're very welcome. It's just that I won't be there.'

'I don't understand.'

'I won't be there. My pupils are teaching the lesson.'

My research took me into many classrooms but that visit to Croydon remains the most peculiar. On my first day investigating effective teaching, there was no teacher to investigate; or rather, there were teachers, but they were 16-year-olds.

The bell rang, Dan walked out and the class filed in. Two of his pupils stood by the whiteboard and introduced the text they'd be studying that day – a passage, rather fittingly, from William Golding's tale of anarchic, self-governing children, *Lord of the Flies*. After about ten minutes, as the pupil-teachers were leading a discussion about the boys' descent into savagery, the Deputy Head eased open the classroom door and snuck inside. He looked around for Dan, frowned, and said: 'Where's Sir?' 'He's not here, Sir,' someone answered, 'We're teaching today.' The Deputy paced around the room, clearly uncertain how to respond, then took a seat at the back.

The lesson was simple but engaging: reading, analysis, work in pairs and whole group discussion, with pupils taking turns to play the teacher's role. The thing that made it interesting for an observer was the atmosphere in the classroom. The pupils were completely focused, passionate even, and extremely mutually supportive. Dan had begun teaching this class at the start of Year 10 and, during that time, he'd fostered an industrious culture that had become so deeply engrained he was confident his pupils would maintain it in the observation without his direct influence.

The bell rang for break time and I waited in the classroom while Dan met with the Deputy. The feedback wasn't great. The Deputy Head had been expecting to see Dan in action and had felt, perhaps unsurprisingly, more like the butt of a practical joke than the privileged witness of a powerful classroom culture. When I asked Dan what he'd been hoping to achieve by his experiment, he explained that he'd put his pupils in charge of the lesson as part of an ongoing effort to boost their confidence and independence, not to imply that pupils learn better without a teacher or to secure a stellar observation rating. Allowing the class to lead a lesson in front of the Deputy Head was, Dan felt, an opportunity to show them his faith in their abilities. 'I'm increasingly drawn to any risk that increases their sense of my belief in them', he said. 'Everything I do is about trying to communicate value – my belief in them – in the hope that they'll internalise it . . . I'd like them to not feel at all inhibited by anything really.'

Total abandonment wasn't a strategy I encountered again, but unusual as it was, there was something about that lesson that set the tone for the visits that followed. Many of the teachers I met also took a deep interest in the way their pupils thought about themselves, their learning and their futures, and in the skills their pupils had to affect those things. Talking to these teachers, it was clear that they felt their role extended to developing qualities like confidence, independence and resilience as well as teaching academic content.

Unwilling and unable

'Giving my pupils a piece of work that is challenging causes them not to be willing to try it, not be willing to fail,' said Charlotte, 'and often results in them getting angry, getting upset, behaving badly – just to avoid being perceived a failure basically. That's a really tough thing to get around. If they won't try, then how can you get them to learn and venture into something that they don't already know the answer to?'

I heard versions of Charlotte's quandary time and time again – stories of under-confident, risk averse and poorly motivated pupils – and I heard similar concerns across primary and secondary classrooms. In fact, the same issues that were plaguing primary teachers seemed to exist right through to the top end of secondary school. In Patrick's Year 3 class 'children would get stuck', he said, 'and rather than carry on by themselves, they would start poking me and following me around.' In a similar vein, Andreas was alarmed by the dependence of his Year 7s, with their constant refrains of '*Sir, I don't get it . . .*' and unwillingness to do anything without consulting him: '*Sir, what do I do after I finish paragraph one?* And I would be like, *Well then you go on to paragraph two.* Things that seemed obvious to me, they needed that reassurance.' Deborah told me about her Year 11 French pupils who were 'doing the bare minimum' and had no intention of pushing themselves any further. 'I know that they are very much capable of more than a C,' she said, 'but the attitude is, *Well all I need is a C, so why would I put in anything more? Why would I aim for a B or an A?*' James S expressed similar frustrations about the attitude of his history GCSE pupils. 'Our kids are just so disorganised! I give out pens on a daily basis to Year 11s who have got an exam in a few weeks, and that gets me down – because it's two fingers up, really. Like, *I was up late last night planning your lesson and you've come to the lesson without a pen to engage in any form of anything.*'

As well as tales of apathy, timidity, frustration and disorganisation, I heard about pupils going to significant lengths to evade work they disliked or didn't think they could do. 'I've never known a child to have such negativity towards maths,' said Becky of one pupil, 'and it kind of displays itself in bad behaviour, distraction, asking any question except for something that's relevant.' Mark talked about a pupil who struggles with literacy but tries to conceal it. 'The problem behind all of his behaviour', he explained, 'was that he can't read and he doesn't know what's going on. He has developed a huge range of strategies for making sure that nobody will ever find out that he can't read. Some of those strategies include misbehaviour.'

These kinds of situations are not uncommon, particularly (but by no means uniquely) in schools in the poorest areas: vicious cycles of low confidence, unwillingness to engage, and underachievement. For Kayleigh, there's a brutal logic to this process: 'If you don't feel confident, you are not going to push yourself to go further. If you can't set yourself aims, you are never going to move forward.' Professor Dylan Wiliam echoes Kayleigh's point: 'The most important instructional decisions are not made by teachers – they are made by students. When students believe they cannot learn, when challenging tasks are just one more opportunity to find out that you are not very smart, many students disengage. And this is perfectly understandable.'[1]

Executive malfunction

I encountered my own versions of these challenges when I was a Year 3 teacher: a pupil who regularly burst into tears during maths lessons, before she'd even attempted the work in front of her; pupils who would hand in three slapdash sentences after twenty minutes of independent writing; others who would try to disrupt, distract, delay – anything to evade the task in hand. It can be frustrating trying to support young people who seem determined to act in opposition to their own interests, and difficult to know how to break down barriers that are, at least partly, inside their heads.

What lies behind all this? Why do so many young people have a block around academic work? A major reason, as Dylan Wiliam suggests, is that past experience has taught them not to bother: that when they try they don't succeed, and that it's better to avoid effort than risk failure. But what leads them to this impasse? There are many possible, potentially interconnected, causes: a lack of essential knowledge and skills; a school culture with low expectations; a family or community with a negative view of education; the pressures and distractions of modern childhood; a sudden transition from a comfortable situation to something unfamiliar. One pupil I spoke to had been quite happy at school until he was required to do extended periods of independent work. 'Now with working by ourselves', he told me, 'I can't do it so I don't like it.' One potential cause to spell out in greater detail – because it brings with it an assortment of complications – is growing up in a highly stressful environment. 'One of the chief insights that the neurobiological research provides', writes Paul Tough, 'is that the behavior of young people, especially young people who have experienced significant adversity, is often under the sway of emotional and psychological and hormonal forces within them that are far from rational.'[2]

When they're very young, children normally develop several foundational skills (collectively known as 'executive function'), which are essential for their concentration and self-control later in life. They learn:

- To decide what to pay attention to and when to shift their attention elsewhere
- To set priorities and control their impulses
- To hold and manipulate information in their working memory

'Children aren't born with these skills', according to a paper by the Harvard Center on the Developing Child, 'they are born with the potential to develop them. If children do not get what they need from their relationships with adults and the conditions in their environments – or (worse) if those influences are sources of toxic stress – their skill development can be seriously delayed or impaired.'[3] Children do not develop these skills automatically and can grow up without them, racking up a range of complications as a consequence – including, frequently, challenging behaviour. 'Scientists who study executive function skills', states another Harvard paper, 'refer to them as the biological foundation for school readiness. They argue that strong working memory, cognitive self-control, and attentional skills provide the basis upon which children's abilities to learn to read, write, and do math can be built.'[4] Clearly, then, lacking these skills is likely to create major challenges in the classroom. As Tough puts it:

> Neurocognitive dysfunctions can quickly become academic dysfunctions. Students don't learn to read on time because it is harder for them to concentrate on the words on the page. They don't learn the basics of number sense because they are too distracted by the emotions and anxieties overloading their nervous systems. As academic material becomes more complicated, they fall behind. As they fall behind, they feel worse about themselves and worse about school. That creates more stress, which often feeds into behavior problems, which leads, in the classroom, to stigmatization and punishment, which keeps their stress levels elevated, which makes it still harder to concentrate – and so on, and so on.[5]

The good news is that, with support and the right conditions, executive function can be improved beyond early childhood. According to the Center on the Developing Child 'the network of brain regions responsible for executive function and self-regulation continues to mature through the early 20s, so there is potentially a long window of time to influence those behaviors'.[6] But, again, this doesn't happen automatically and, as children get older, strengthening executive function also involves addressing and unravelling the numerous learning and behavioural issues that may have arisen in the meantime.

Missing links

For some young people, early childhood stress and underdeveloped executive function lie behind their unwillingness or inability to engage, make an effort, and focus on challenging work. For others, there are different reasons. All of which is to say that growing up in the poorest areas can lead to a range of educational challenges that become knotted together and difficult to untie.

What's to be done then? What can we offer young people who seem over-whelmed by low self-belief, frustration and disaffection? There's a growing consensus in the research and policy communities that 'the missing link'[7] for these young people is a set of mindsets and skills that underpin success in learning and in life. Alternately referred to as non-cognitive skills, soft skills, life skills, success skills, social and emotional skills, character traits, character strengths, and often just character, a great deal of hope has been invested in these intangible assets.

Following many conversations with teachers and pupils, this was my conclusion too: that in order to make outstanding academic progress pupils need to develop new ways of thinking about themselves and new ways of approaching their learning. These skills and mindsets have been packaged up and labelled in many different ways, as the list above suggests, but they seem to boil down to three crucial qualities:

- **Confidence:** believing you can succeed, being willing to make an effort, and daring to think ambitiously about the future
- **Independence:** working autonomously, solving your own problems and taking responsibility for your learning
- **Resilience:** pushing yourself, pursuing your aims in the face of challenges, and recovering from setbacks

If pupils feel confident, independent and resilient, and act accordingly, the disengagement and defeatism vanishes. Instead of giving up, avoiding challenge and limiting themselves, young people throw themselves whole-heartedly into their learning, believing they can succeed and equipped with the skills and determination to do so.

Vicious or virtuous

In combination, confidence, independence and resilience kick-start a virtuous cycle of effort, persistence and academic achievement: a small success leads to further effort and persistence, which leads to a slightly bigger success, which leads to greater effort and greater persistence, leading to an even bigger success, and so on, each success inspiring and igniting the next. As pupils accumulate new academic knowledge and skills, their confidence is vindicated and they seek out further challenges. John Hattie and Gregory Yates describe this process as follows:

> The virtuous cycle involves convincing oneself that one might succeed on a task or challenge and thus invest effort, listen and even seek instruction, welcome errors as opportunities to learn, and receive feedback, thus leading to evidence that one was right.[8]

Or as a literature review from the University of Chicago puts it:

> When students value the work they are doing, feel a sense of belonging in the classroom [. . .], feel capable of succeeding, and believe they will master challenging material with effort, they are much more likely to engage in difficult work and see it through to completion.[9]

This pattern of thought and behaviour is the opposite of the vicious cycle described to me by so many teachers. The challenge for teachers, however, is that *both* cycles feel true and inevitable from the inside. Vicious or virtuous, each is a closed circuit with its own self-confirming logic. In Nobel-laureate James Heckman's words: 'Skill begets skill; motivation begets motivation.' But also, he adds: 'Early failure begets later failure'.[10]

Stating the obvious

Is any of this new or surprising? Thinkers from Aristotle onwards have argued that our thoughts and habits affect our actions and achievements. Saying that confidence, independence and resilience have a big impact on young people's learning is a bit like saying that petrol has a big impact on a car's ability to move. These are the qualities we use to achieve *anything* challenging in life – of course they're important to schoolchildren. So why all of the interest and debate now?

'Character' and 'non-cognitive skills' have become hotly debated topics, much mentioned in political speeches and the press (earning a prominent place, for example, in the 2016 government white paper, *Educational Excellence Everywhere*, which stated that schooling should instil 'character traits' that 'help [pupils] succeed: being resilient and knowing how to persevere, how to bounce back if faced with failure, and how to collaborate with others'. These skills, the paper said, 'underpin academic success, happiness and wellbeing').

The reason that this subject has been thrust into the spotlight in recent years is the emergence of new insights from psychology and neuroscience. This new research promises to add rigour and clarity to what can sometimes seem like an opaque and intangible subject. Thus far:

1   **It has confirmed the critical importance of certain mindsets and skills,** suggesting that they can be as, if not more, predictive of academic success than measures of cognitive ability
2   **It has given us greater clarity on the relative malleability of those mindsets and skills**

3   **It has reinforced the view that a deficit in these qualities is a significant factor in the educational achievement gap** between children from rich and poor backgrounds. (For a summary of the research evidence see Chapter 9, p.118)

These findings, transmitted in a spate of recent books and reports (see p.137 for a list of significant publications), have lent a legitimacy and urgency to this debate and led educationalists to question why we aren't dedicating more attention to this area, and to pursue new evidence-based avenues in the way we approach it.

Psyched up

The essence of much of this new research is that we need to pay careful attention to the psychology of the young people we teach and to recognise that we shape our pupils' thoughts and behaviours through our classroom culture, dialogue, relationships, routines and instruction, whether we're aware of it or not. Over time, these thoughts and behaviours take root and, for better or worse, become habits.

'When we refer to the psychology of the student, what do we mean?' write Professors Dweck, Walton and Cohen in their paper on 'Academic Tenacity'. 'We mean that students need to think of themselves and school in certain ways in order to want to learn and in order to learn successfully. We also mean that they are able to regulate themselves in ways that promote learning. When these non-cognitive factors are in place, students will look – and be – motivated.'[11]

To continue the car analogy, if you devote all of your time to souping-up the engine but forget to fill up the tank, you won't get anywhere. Psychologists have been at pains recently to make a similarly basic, and similarly crucial, point about learning: academic progress depends not only on intelligence, but on what young people do with it. Your pupils' success depends on *what they actually do every day*: the way they work and the amount of effort they invest, and those things are determined by how confident, independent and resilient they are. As Dweck, Walton and Cohen put it:

> Academic success requires more than ability. It requires the application of ability and the growth of ability through sustained hard work. Mindsets, goals, and self-regulatory skills [. . .] play key roles in this enterprise.[12]

The encouraging finding for teachers working with pupils who seem to be caught in a self-defeating spiral of under-confidence and underachievement, is that these are precisely the young people who tend to benefit most from explicit support in this area. 'The lowest-performing and most at-risk students are thought to be the hardest to reach', write Dweck, Walton and Cohen but, in fact, 'they often respond *most* to these kinds of interventions' because 'in many cases these non-cognitive factors were holding them back.'[13] This is a tantalising statement: the very pupils that teachers were describing to me, young people from poor backgrounds who seemed particularly blocked, are in fact the young people most likely to make rapid, even life-changing, improvements if we can give them the right kind of support.

What next?

It's an exciting time. There's a clear consensus that a lack of non-cognitive, or 'character', skills is holding back a group of young people who are struggling academically, and that developing those mindsets and skills would greatly improve their academic engagement and performance. And yet, this is where the agreement ends. There's no equivalent consensus over how to develop character and non-cognitive skills, or even how far that's possible. Debate rages around how malleable these qualities are, how they develop, and in what context we should try to develop them. This conundrum – *What can we change? How? And where?* – is the next frontier for teachers, researchers and policy makers.

To date, a lot of the research into developing character and non-cognitive skills has focused on interventions that take place on the fringes of children's schooling: one-off workshops or series of workshops; extra-curricular activities; trips and residential courses. By contrast, relatively little has been published about what teachers can do during lesson time, without siphoning time away from academic learning or finding extra hours in the day. This is despite the fact that major reports have expressed optimism about the impact teachers could have within their day-to-day practice. 'With greater awareness of non-cognitive factors,' write Dweck, Walton and Cohen, 'educators may be able to do relatively small things in the classroom that can make a big difference in their students' learning.'[14]

I asked Dan how the culture in his Year 11 class developed, and how the group had come to be so confident and driven. 'No one wants to fail,' he said. 'When they come into the classroom, if you make them believe that they are going to succeed and you give them the tools to do so, then they will.' Dan makes this sound rather straightforward. But is it? What can teachers actually do to tackle and replace self-defeating outlooks and habits with self-propelling confidence, independence and resilience?

Trade-offs

I used to show video case studies of classrooms my team visited to groups of trainee teachers. They took a particular interest in how, and whether, teachers can affect outcomes beyond the academic. 'How do you go about concretely teaching non-cognitive skills?' I was asked frequently. 'Can you focus on these things and still get the grades?' Many new teachers I spoke to found this area confusing and problematic. They earnestly wanted their pupils to be confident, independent and resilient, but were understandably concerned about trying to squeeze yet another set of objectives and activities into limited lesson time and onto their bulging to do lists.

At the time, I had hunches, but I didn't have a clear answer for them. Lesson time is always tight and there are few things as endless as a teacher's to do list. With so much to do already – with so many good, meaningful things to do – is this area really a priority? If you're working with pupils who are already behind academically, is focusing on non-cognitive skills *as well* a trade-off you should make?

Over the course of my observations and interviews, I took a particular interest in these questions and, as it happened, many of the teachers I encountered were similarly intrigued by this area and had begun exploring how to work on it. As such, even as I was reading blogs, press articles and academic papers describing a general uncertainty around how to develop character and non-cognitive skills, I was going on visits that strongly suggested that there are things that teachers can do, in the course of their day-to-day teaching – often 'relatively small things', to echo Dweck, Walton and Cohen – that have a big influence on their pupils' confidence, independence and resilience.

The very teachers who were working with most vigour and innovation tended to be the teachers who described the most intractable-sounding issues in their classrooms. They would tell me about their pupils' low self-belief and fear of failure, then go on to outline the changes they had made to their day-to-day teaching practice: tangible ways to develop intangible-sounding mindsets and skills. Their actions included normalising and celebrating mistake-making as part of learning; talking to pupils about the importance of a growth mindset; using feedback to highlight small steps and encourage greater effort; teaching pupils techniques to use when they are stuck; talking frankly to their pupils about the relationship between the classroom and their future lives; allowing pupils to choose the difficulty level of their work and push themselves; creating environments in which pupils who lack 'executive function' skills can develop them. Katie, a secondary science teacher, made it her mission 'to challenge the paradigms that are stuck in [pupils'] heads' and are 'so entrenched that they're not conscious.' Sam, teaching Year 2, was determined to 'show [pupils] the progress they are making' so that 'they know that they can be successful.' Elizabeth, teaching Year 1, wanted her pupils to realise that 'if [they] don't take risks, [they] will never learn anything'. Overall, the teachers I observed demanded their pupils' best work in every single lesson, even as they used their classroom routines, relationships, dialogue and instruction to foster the skills, mindsets and habits that would enable pupils to produce it.

As I studied what these teachers were doing, and the things that they and their pupils said to me, one of the first things that became clear was that the trade-off the trainee teachers were worried about doesn't exist. You can pursue academic learning *and* increased confidence, independence and resilience simultaneously, with each element reinforcing the other: you build confidence by supporting pupils to tackle and overcome academic challenges; build independence by giving them ever greater ownership of their learning; and develop resilience by equipping them with strategies to deal with failure and persevere. Academic work is an ideal arena for developing these non-academic outcomes. The teachers I observed hadn't found lots of extra time or compromised their curriculum. On the contrary, they were being efficient: making the most of every lesson with young people by working on two sets of mutually-reinforcing outcomes at once. Confidence, independence and resilience activate effort, help pupils to overcome and recover from challenges, and, ultimately, enable learning. By combining these two sets of aims you stand to increase, not jeopardise, pupil achievement.

Learning from primary and secondary classrooms around the country I was struck afresh by the power of treating teachers, in Doug Lemov's words, 'not just as recipients and implementers of the field's knowledge but as creators of it'. 'We are not suffering from a lack of solutions', he continues, 'so much as our failure to learn from teachers who have generated insight and put their ideas to work.'[15] Combining ground-level investigations with existing academic research, I began to assemble a framework of pupil outcomes and a model to support teachers to address them, documenting the practical ideas I'd witnessed in classrooms.

Unravelling the character conundrum

The 2016 *Building Blocks for Learning* report by Turnaround for Children ends by saying that 'the gap between theory and practice regarding the development and support of these skills and mindsets remains large' and that 'a critical piece of the work ahead' is 'identifying and codifying practice that effectively addresses student development and its integration with academics, particularly in environments with high concentrations of students facing adversity.'[16] Similarly, Paul Tough ends his 2016 book *Helping Children Succeed* by saying that 'as the value of non-cognitive skills has become more widely acknowledged, demand has grown for a curriculum or a textbook or a teaching strategy to guide us in helping students develop these skills.'[17] This book is an attempt to fill these gaps: to unravel the character conundrum and provide teachers with a guide to developing their pupils' confidence, independence and resilience within and through their day-to-day teaching.

Although this guide is full of practical techniques, the approach outlined here is as much about looking freshly at what you do already as it is about doing new and different things. The key to this approach is being deliberate and consistent: knowing which mindsets, skills and habits you're trying to develop, and planning out the details of your classroom culture, relationships, routines and instruction so that they align and combine to address your aims. You may be doing some of the things suggested in this guide already but, depending on how you do them and how you talk about them, they may not be making a difference to pupils' confidence, independence and resilience. As well as offering new ideas, therefore, this guide is a lens through which to examine your current practice and consider whether, with relatively small adjustments, your teaching could be addressing a broader range of outcomes. To quote Lemov again: 'Often very small changes can have large and profound effects on big problems.'[18]

Given the gaps in existing research, this book does not claim to be comprehensive, definitive, or even totally correct. The field of character and non-cognitive skills is rapidly evolving and the coming years will see many new insights from academic studies and individual classrooms and schools. However, I hope that the approach outlined here sparks further debate and, most importantly, supports teachers to break vicious cycles and give pupils the mindsets, skills and habits they need to succeed.

Notes

1 Wiliam, D. (2013). Assessment: the bridge between teaching and learning. *Voices from the Middle*, 21(2), p.19.
2 Tough, P. (2016). *Helping Children Succeed: What Works and Why*. 1st ed. [PDF], p.67. Available at: paultough.com/helping.
3 Center on the Developing Child. (2012). *Executive Function* (InBrief). Retrieved from www.developingchild.harvard.edu
4 Center on the Developing Child at Harvard University. (2011). *Building the Brain's "Air Traffic Control" System: How Early Experiences Shape the Development of Executive Function: Working Paper No. 11*. p.4.
5 Tough, P. (2016). *Helping Children Succeed: What Works and Why*. 1st ed. [PDF], p.82.

6 Center on the Developing Child at Harvard University. (2016). *Building Core Capabilities for Life: The Science Behind the Skills Adults Need to Succeed in Parenting and in the Workplace.* p.9.

7 All-Party Parliamentary Group on Social Mobility. (2012). 'Seven Key Truths about Social Mobility' Interim Report.

8 Hattie, J. and Yates, G. (2013). *Visible Learning and the Science of How We Learn.* Abingdon: Routledge, p.224.

9 Farrington, C.A., Roderick, M., Allensworth, E., Nagaoka, J., Keyes, T.S., Johnson, D.W., and Beechum, N.O. (2012). *Teaching Adolescents to Become Learners. The Role of Noncognitive Factors in Shaping School Performance: A Critical Literature Review.* Chicago: University of Chicago Consortium on Chicago School Research, p.26.

10 Heckman, J. (2006). The economics of investing in children. UCD Geary Institute: *Evidence Policy Briefing* (1), p.3.

11 Dweck, C., Walton, G., and Cohen, G. (2011). *Academic Tenacity: Mindsets and Skills that Promote Long-Term Learning.* Seattle, WA: The Gates Foundation, p.2.

12 ibid. p.13.

13 ibid. p.5.

14 ibid. p.3.

15 Lemov, D. (2015). *Teach Like a Champion 2.0.* San Francisco: Jossey-Bass, p.8.

16 Stafford-Brizard, B. (2016). *Building Blocks for Learning: A Framework for Comprehensive Student Development.* Turnaround for Children, p.9.

17 Tough, P. (2016). *Helping Children Succeed: What Works and Why.* 1st ed. [PDF], p.15.

18 Lemov, D. (2015). *Teach Like a Champion 2.0.* San Francisco: Jossey-Bass, p.10.

THIS BOOK AT A GLANCE

Confidence, independence and resilience are hugely important

- Confidence, independence and resilience make an enormous difference to pupils' academic progress, and to their wellbeing and opportunities long term.

They can be developed by teachers in the classroom

- Confidence, independence and resilience are useful umbrella terms, which encapsulate a range of specific skills, mindsets and habits.
- Teachers can develop these skills, mindsets and habits through their classroom culture, dialogue, relationships, routines and instruction.
- Some skills and mindsets are known to be malleable. Where that's not the case, or there isn't sufficient evidence, pupils can still develop strategies and habits that allow them to act *as though they have* a particular mindset or skill.

Teachers can plan for progress in this area, as they would for academic learning

- To make the greatest impact, teachers need clear aims and a deliberate, structured approach for addressing those aims day-to-day.
- Assessment is critical for both understanding and accelerating impact in this area. The greater the pupil involvement in the assessment process, the more powerful it becomes.

Focusing on confidence, independence and resilience isn't at odds with academic learning

- Developing these skills and mindsets shouldn't detract from academic work. In fact, by focusing on academic and non-academic outcomes simultaneously, teachers can equip their pupils with powerful habits that accelerate academic progress.

- The main way that pupils develop confidence, independence and resilience in the classroom is by attempting difficult work and experiencing academic success. The process of investing effort, overcoming challenges and experiencing success can become a self-propelling cycle.

We still have a lot to learn

- There is plenty of evidence to say that confidence, independence and resilience matter for pupils, but less evidence describing how best to develop them in the classroom, or how to evaluate progress.
- This is an emerging area, in which teachers can actively participate by testing new ideas and sharing what they learn.

Navigating this book

This book falls into two loose halves. In the first half you'll find all the background you need to access this area and address it in the classroom. You'll find:

- An overview of the debates around 'character' in the **Introduction (p.x)**;
- A framework of pupil outcomes and success criteria in **Our aims for pupils (p.1)**;
- An explanation of the overall approach to this area, including a flowchart of teacher actions (p.18), in **Developing confidence, independence and resilience in the classroom (p.15)**;
- And two case studies – one primary, one secondary – showing what this approach looks like in practice in **Case Study: Year 2 (p.23)** and **Case Study: Year 9 French (p.28)**.

The second half of the book contains a step-by-step guide to applying this approach in your own classroom. You'll find practical strategies and concrete examples to support you to apply the three stages of the teacher flowchart:

- **Knowing where you're going (p.36)**;
- **Creating the right conditions (p.46)**;
- **Building new habits (p.71)**.

The book closes with a short section describing the value of **Learning from other phases and subjects (p.109)** and a section **Exploring the evidence (p.112)** underpinning the pupil outcomes listed in this guide.

Although it may be tempting to jump straight to the practical strategies and ideas, you'll get far more out of these sections if you spend time, in the first half of the book, exploring the debates in this lively, contentious field and considering your overall aims and approach.

1 Our aims for pupils

Word problems

Given the clear consensus that certain basic mindsets and skills underpin academic success, and that they are in short supply for many young people, it's surprising how little agreement there is around what to call this set of aims and how to talk about them. Read around the subject and you encounter an impressive variety of competing, seemingly interchangeable, labels: non-cognitive skills, non-cognitive factors, non-academic skills, soft skills, life skills, success skills, social and emotional skills, performance virtues, academic tenacity, character traits, character skills, character strengths, and often just character. Of all of them, 'character' and 'non-cognitive skills' lead the pack, and yet neither of these two, nor any of the others, quite work. In this area, the terminology itself is a conundrum, more often clouding than clarifying meaning, and perhaps this is why there are so many terms in circulation, and why fresh alternatives are constantly being coined.

Does it matter which words we use? We get the gist, and perhaps the imprecisions of 'character' and 'non-cognitive skills' are preferable to semantic nit-picking. And yet, there are real problems with some of this language, problems that impede and distort our communication. As the critic Raymond Williams put it, many concepts cannot 'really be thought through, and some of them [. . .] cannot even be focused on unless we are conscious of the words as elements of the problems.'[1]

Perhaps the big villain here is 'character', with its overtones of Victorian sturdiness and stiff upper lips. 'The trouble is character sounds very moralistic', says Professor James Heckman. 'It sounds like we're running a Sunday School.'[2] Nevertheless, Heckman suggests we stick with it, as do Richard Reeves and Joanna Venator, authors with Kimberly Howard of the 2014 report, 'The Character Factor.' 'Don't back away from using the term character, which is the clearest overall label: just be specific what you mean when you talk about it.'[3]

Their desire to cling to the term is understandable, but unfortunately the word is tinged with the upper-class values of a different age – an uncomfortable resonance in discussions about the education of children from the poorest backgrounds today. This resonance is all the more unfortunate because it occasionally leads to the mistaken assumption that academics and policymakers are accusing the poorest young people of lacking character and grittiness in a more general sense, and to retorts that growing up in adversity gives a person far more character than sitting in a comfortable office. Distracting arguments of this kind are one consequence of inapt terminology.

An even more serious issue with the word character is the air of immutability it communicates. The general impression that the word 'character' conveys is that you've got it or you haven't. Heckman suggests the term 'character skills' (as opposed to traits) to suggest malleability. Reeves and Venator suggest 'character strengths'. But these modifiers don't sufficiently distance us from the idea that your character is something you're born with, or from the idea that character refers to a person's whole personality, not a specific subset of mindsets and skills. Given the broader meaning of the term character in general parlance, it's understandable that some people become wary when they hear talk of 'character development' in schools and imagine something closer to brain washing than confidence building. All in all, then, 'character' provokes an array of unhelpful associations and leads us down a variety of argumentative cul de sacs. We're not talking about meddling with the essence of someone's being or imposing upper-class values on working-class children; we're talking about helping young people develop a range of basic skills and mindsets, which are essential for their success in school and beyond. The word character does not communicate this simply or clearly enough.

'Non-cognitive skills', ostensibly more neat and scientific, is not much better. Many psychologists have rubbished the term, describing it as nonsensical at best and dangerously misleading at worst. The University of Chicago literature review puts it like this:

> [W]e find "noncognitive" to be an unfortunate word. It reinforces a false dichotomy between what comes to be perceived as weightier, more academic "cognitive" factors and what by comparison becomes perceived as a separate category of fluffier "noncognitive" or "soft" skills. As others have pointed out, contrasting cognitive and noncognitive factors can be confusing because "few aspects of human behavior are devoid of cognition" [...] How could one's study skills, for example, not be part of a cognitive process?[4]

There is simply no such thing as a 'non-cognitive skill'; all of our skills are the product of cognition. And, as such, this term encourages unhelpful ways of talking to pupils about how they think and learn, and encourages teachers to fence off the acquisition of academic knowledge from the acquisition of the skills and mindsets that underpin academic learning. For Reeves, Venator and Howard, the problem is the breadth and unspecificity of this term: 'The problem is that it is too broad, lumping together a very wide range of skills, traits and attributes – from stable aspects of personality through to everyday social skills.'[5]

And so, both 'character' and 'non-cognitive skills', the two most common labels for these skills and mindsets, have serious flaws. For this reason, people working on this area tend either to use them with caveats, or to invent new terms of their own. Neither approach is ideal and it may be time to call off the search for a single overarching label. Instead, I'd propose naming the specific outcomes we're interested in: **confidence**, **independence** and **resilience**. Although these are still umbrella terms, they are more focused and transparent than most of the designations listed above.

Value judgements

Before defining confidence, independence and resilience and diving into our aims for pupils in more detail, it's worth pausing to consider how they fit within the broader spectrum of aims we might have for a young person's education. One of the chief criticisms of the character and non-cognitive skills debate is how narrow, mechanistic, even self-centred, outcomes like confidence, independence and resilience can seem. Don't we want to foster good citizens with strong values? Why aren't we talking about gratitude, generosity, humility and compassion as well?

In a review of David Brooks's 2015 book *The Road to Character*, Rowan Williams made an impassioned case against 'the bland managerialism that is replacing discussion about the core values of our educational system'. We may wish young people to have self-control and resilience, Williams continues, but our vision for young people should not be 'a style of living that accepts limits and deferrals' but rather 'the kind of vision that makes sense of limits and deferrals, that would make struggle and frustration worthwhile.' In other words, unless we support pupils to consider what is worth struggling for in life, rather than simply teaching them how to persevere and be self-controlled, our educational philosophy risks becoming 'functionalist and reductive'. '"Character" without solidarity, and so without compassion and a principled universal perspective on human dignity,' Williams concludes, 'can be yet another stalking horse for self-regard and self-protection.'[6]

These are wise words and it's true that the qualities most often discussed in the current conversations about character and non-cognitive skills tend to be functional and performance-related: skills and mindsets that underpin individual effort and perseverance, rather than moral values or virtues that involve looking outward. There are, however, good reasons for the narrowness of this discussion. The first is that a lack of certain functional mindsets, skills and habits is preventing many pupils from learning successfully; we urgently need to understand this area better and ensure that all pupils can approach learning and life with confidence, independence and resilience. A second reason is that focusing on these non-negotiable mindsets and skills doesn't negate the importance of other qualities and values, or suggest that schools don't have an important responsibility in that regard too. Needless to say, decency, generosity, humility and gratitude will shape the way in which more functional skills and mindsets are employed.

This book is specifically focused on how to support pupils, especially pupils from the poorest backgrounds, to overcome a particular, and particularly pervasive, barrier to learning. But the book's tight scope should not be read as a statement that these are the *only* personal qualities that matter for young people. Bigger questions of values, citizenship and a life well lived should be at the heart of every child's education, defined and debated by families, schools and communities together.

Confidence, independence and resilience

Pupils need three qualities to engage in learning and succeed academically: confidence, independence and resilience. These are broad aims – the product of numerous specific mindsets, skills and habits – and teachers need a clear idea of what they mean and how they break down into smaller, more tangible outcomes. This section defines these overarching concepts and maps out the steps pupils need to take to become confident, independent, resilient learners.

Confidence

Confidence is to do with trust and reliance. In the classroom context, it's about your pupils' faith in themselves - how they perceive themselves and their abilities - and it affects their willingness to participate or make an effort. Whenever the word confidence appears in this guide it means: **believing you can succeed, being willing to try and take risks, and daring to think ambitiously about the future.**

Independence

Independence is about thinking and acting autonomously. When the word appears in this guide it means: **working autonomously, solving your own problems, and taking responsibility for your learning.**

Resilience

Resilience is originally a scientific term describing how well a material recovers its shape after being put under pressure. This is a useful image for the way the word is used in this guide: **pushing yourself, recovering from setbacks, and pursuing your aims in the face of challenges.**

Mapping out pupil outcomes

At its very simplest, the journey from lacking to having confidence, independence and resilience looks like this:

	Confidence	*Independence*	*Resilience*
Stage 1: Growing in positivity and willingness to participate	– Lacking in confidence	– Dependent on the teacher	– Giving up when challenged
Stage 2: Taking risks in a safe environment	– Tentative confidence within a positive, trusting classroom culture	– Simulating independence using class systems and routines	– Willing to persist at challenging work within a structured, supportive environment
Stage 3: Seeking out challenge and taking ownership of learning	– Growing in genuine confidence based on overcoming challenges and experiencing success	– Increasingly able to work without explicit structure and support, taking ownership of learning	– Willing and able to persevere and overcome challenges in pursuit of ambitious aims

For pupils to move from one stage to the next, they need to acquire a range of specific mindsets, skills and habits. The flowchart below (Figure 1.1) maps out the different outcomes for pupils at each of these three stages, showing how they seem to interact and the sequence in which they seem to develop. The outcomes are grouped into mindsets (how pupils think and feel), habits (how pupils normally act) and metacognitive strategies (practical, learnable skills that pupils can use to support themselves – for more information on this term see p.124). After the flowchart, you'll find a list of explanatory statements, detailing what each of the outcomes looks like in practice.

This outcomes flowchart is an amalgamation of both my team's classroom research and major academic papers and literature reviews (for more on the evidence base see p.118). Although there's new research emerging all the time, I believe there's value in taking what we think we know and arranging it in a form that supports teachers' work in classrooms now.

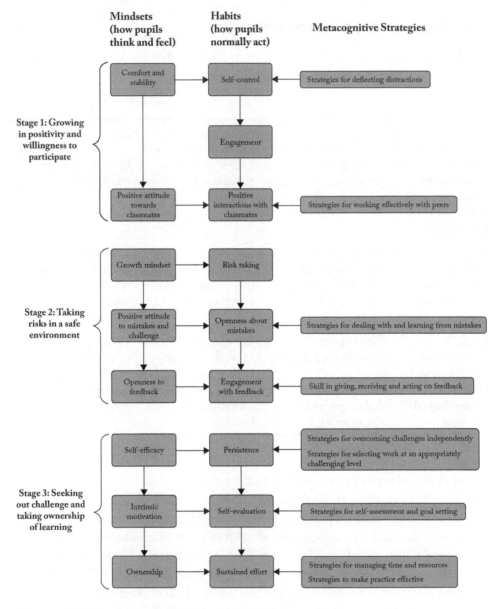

Figure 1.1 Pupil outcomes flowchart

An essential point to keep in mind as you look at this chart is that the mindsets, skills and habits outlined here don't develop in isolation, either from academic work or from one another. As the EEF Literature Review puts it:

> There is no single non-cognitive skill that predicts long-term outcomes. Rather key skills are inter-related and need to be developed in combination with each other.[7]

One of the main challenges when working on these outcomes, therefore, is being aware of the contingencies and connections between them. The arrows here suggest the links between outcomes and the flow from one to the next; in reality, there are more relationships between these outcomes than it's possible or useful to represent.

Success criteria

The aim of this flowchart is to enable you to think through what it means for pupils to be confident, independent and resilient, and to show you the steps they need to take to get there. Below you'll find success criteria for each outcome on the chart, describing what you'll see and hear if pupils have developed a new mindset or habit.

The flowchart and success criteria can be used:

- To reflect on your pupils' starting points;
- To guide your planning;
- To support your evaluation (for more on the planning and evaluation process see p.36);
- And to provide a common language to discuss these aims with pupils (see p.61).

Comfort and stability

- I feel safe and comfortable in this classroom
- I trust my teacher
- My teacher knows us and cares about us
- My teacher sets us work we can do
- My teacher believes in us and encourages us
- My teacher is interested in our opinions
- I enjoy coming to this class

Positive attitude towards classmates

- We're a team in this classroom
- We can all learn from one another

Positive interactions with classmates

- I work well with others
- I support others and seek their support when I need it

Self-control

- I ignore distractions and resist impulses
- I pay attention to what we're doing

Engagement

- I arrive punctually
- I participate actively in lessons

Growth mindset

- I know that intelligence isn't fixed
- I believe I can improve with effort and practice

Risk taking

- I have a go at things even if they look difficult

Positive attitude to mistakes and challenge

- Mistakes are an important part of learning
- I'm not embarrassed about making mistakes
- Challenging work helps me learn

Openness about mistakes

- I share my mistakes so that others can learn from them

Openness to feedback

- I can see the progress I'm making
- Good feedback lets me know what I'm doing well and what I need to do to improve
- I can get useful feedback from adults or from other pupils

Engagement with feedback

- I pay attention to feedback and act on it
- I give feedback to other pupils and receive feedback from them
- I regularly take stock of my progress

Self-efficacy

- When I try hard at challenging work I do well at it
- I know what I need to do to succeed at a task
- I can deal with setbacks

Persistence

- I keep going when I'm struggling
- I use strategies to help myself
- I seek out the resources I need
- I only ask the teacher for help when I've exhausted all other options
- I complete pieces of independent work

Intrinsic motivation

- This class matters to me
- I have dreams for my future
- I know how day-to-day work connects to the future
- I'm determined to succeed
- I like to push myself

Self-evaluation

- I seek out feedback and use it to improve
- I monitor my own progress
- I set goals for myself

Ownership

- I'm responsible for my learning
- I know how I'm doing and how to improve

Sustained effort

- I can prioritise long term aims over short term desires
- I seek out challenging work
- I organise my time and my materials
- I work hard outside of lessons
- I do deliberate practice to improve
- I keep going over long periods and in the face of setbacks

Virtuous cycles

What the pupil outcomes flowchart doesn't adequately communicate is the iterative, cyclical nature of this process: effort leads to success, which leads to confidence, which leads to more effort, which leads to more success, more confidence, and so on. Throughout the process, you're constantly pushing pupils to reinvest the confidence, resilience and independence they've gained, in order to increase them further and make even greater progress.

As discussed on p.xvii, this cycle arises frequently in the literature around this area. The University of Chicago review states that there is 'a reciprocal relationship among mindsets, perseverance, behaviors, and performance. Strong

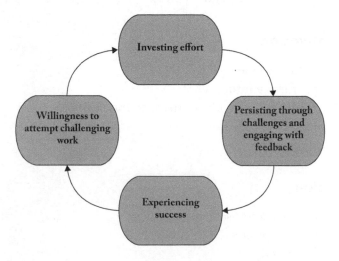

Figure 1.2 Virtuous cycle

academic performance "validates" positive mindsets, increases perseverance, and reinforces strong academic behaviors.'[8]

The skills and mindsets in stages 1 and 2 of the outcomes chart are prerequisites for setting this process in motion. Once these foundations are in place, teachers can catalyse a virtuous cycle (see Figure 1.2) through which pupils – in stage 3 – begin to drive their own academic progress and foster their own confidence, independence and resilience.

What can we actually change?

Before moving on to the next section, about how to develop your pupils' confidence, independence and resilience in the classroom, we should address the question of how malleable the outcomes in this flowchart are: what we know teachers can actually change.

The short answer is that you can have a significant influence on the outcomes outlined in the flowchart. In *Academic Tenacity: Mindsets and Skills that Promote Long-Term Learning*, Dweck, Walton and Cohen write that '[s]ome students bring these mindsets and skills with them to school, but these mindsets and skills can also be taught.'[9] Likewise, in their 2013 literature review, *The Impact of Non-Cognitive Skills on Outcomes for Young People*, the Education Endowment Foundation concluded that '[w]ithin school, effective teaching, the school environment, and social and emotional learning programmes (SEL) can play an important role in developing key non-cognitive skills.'[10] This isn't to say that pupils don't arrive with different strengths, experiences and inclinations, but rather that the particular skills, mindsets and habits that make pupils feel and act confident, independent and resilient can be affected by what happens in the classrooms.

There is particularly strong evidence for the malleability of certain outcomes. For example, Carol Dweck's research has shown that growth mindset – a belief that intelligence isn't fixed and can be improved with effort – can be developed in pupils within a relatively short time frame. In the words of Angela Duckworth, 'maladaptive, incorrect beliefs about skill development and achievement' can be intentionally changed:

> For instance, individuals who believe that frustration and confusion mean they should quit what they are doing may be taught that these emotions are common during the learning process. Likewise, individuals who believe that mistakes are to be avoided at all costs may be taught that the most effective form of practice [. . .] entails tackling challenges beyond one's current skill level.[11]

Beliefs, attitudes, self-perception and motivations can change – an exciting prospect when you consider, as Hattie and Yates put it, that 'our beliefs about our learning can inhibit further learning'.[12] Likewise, practical skills for supporting yourself in the classroom – 'when you know what to do when you don't know what to do',[13] in Hattie's words – are definitely learnable. The EEF review calls these types of skills 'meta-cognitive strategies' and is confident that they are important and malleable:

> There is clear evidence that meta-cognitive strategies are malleable and can be taught or otherwise developed in students from primary school to university and across a wide range of academic subjects. They have also been shown to have medium to large effects on a number of academic outcomes.[14]

The most contentious outcomes in this guide, with regard to malleability, are 'persistence' and 'sustained effort': the outcomes to do with resilience. There is ongoing debate around how far we can influence a person's resolve and sticking power; according to researchers at the Harvard Center on the Developing Child, 'resilience is shaped throughout life by the accumulation of experiences – both good and bad – and the continuing development of adaptive coping skills connected to those experiences. What happens early may matter most, but it is never too late to build resilience.'[15] In other words, you can become more or less resilient, but this is something that happens over time, through experience. 'Self-control' also falls into this camp. The EEF review puts it like this: 'Some non-cognitive skills including 'grit' [not a standalone outcome here; see p.126] and self-control correlate strongly with outcomes but appear to be more akin to stable personality traits rather than to malleable skills.'[16]

Nevertheless, regardless of how malleable resilience and self-control are, and over what time frames, there are things teachers can do to help pupils *act* in more resilient, self-controlled ways. By overturning unhelpful mindsets, teaching new skills and encouraging new habits, teachers can make it more likely that pupils will try to resist distractions, control their impulses and persist with challenging work, and ensure that they have the metacognitive strategies to do so meaningfully.

The University of Chicago's literature review expands on this notion, stating that teachers can support all pupils to act with greater perseverance, *regardless of how malleable perseverance may be*. They can do this by focusing on developing 'positive mindsets' and 'metacognitive and self-regulatory skills' that enable pupils to exhibit 'greater perseverance and better academic behaviors':

> While some students are more likely to persist in tasks or exhibit self-discipline than others, *all* students are more likely to demonstrate

perseverance if the school or classroom context helps them develop positive mindsets and effective learning strategies. In other words, the mechanisms through which teachers can lead students to exhibit greater perseverance and better academic behaviors in their classes are through attention to academic mindsets and development of students' metacognitive and self-regulatory skills, rather than trying to change their innate tendency to persevere.[17]

The nuance here is quite fine, but it's an important one: the question of malleability matters but, whatever the answer, it doesn't prevent teachers from supporting pupils to approach their work with greater confidence, independence and resilience. This is significant, the report makes clear, because academic behaviours – *the things pupils actually do* – 'have the most immediate effect on students' course grades.'[18] If research demonstrates that a given quality isn't very malleable, the teacher has still taught their pupils tangible strategies and habits that enable them to act *as though they have it*. It may be that we can't quickly affect a pupil's levels of resilience, but we can definitely equip them with skills and mindsets that improve their ability and willingness to persevere with challenging work. If, on the other hand, we begin with the premise that certain skills are innate and unalterable, we immediately put a cap on what pupils might achieve and the lengths to which we might go to support them. The ultimate aim of this guide is to support you to catalyse enduring change in pupils' mindsets and skills; in the absence of firm evidence about malleability, the starting point is enabling you to establish concrete habits that improve pupil performance day-to-day.

Another unresolved issue, according to the EEF, is the extent to which 'skills can be transferred between areas of a young person's life, and how far changes can be sustained in the long term.'[19] These are important questions, whose answers have major implications for pupil outcomes, but they too are no impediment to teachers getting to work. Pupils need these skills, mindsets and habits every day in the classroom; if they endure and transfer across contexts and over time, all the better. As evidence accrues, teachers will be able to select teaching methods that support longevity and transferability. For now, further research is required to establish exactly what they are.

Notes

1 Williams, R. (2014). *Keywords*. 1st ed. London: Fourth Estate, p.16. [original – Fontana 1983].
2 Heckman, J. (2012). Back to School. *This American Life* [Podcast]. 14 September 2012. Available at: www.thisamericanlife.org/radio-archives/episode/474/back-to-school

3 Reeves, R. and Venator, J. (2014). Jingle-Jangle Fallacies for Non-Cognitive Factors. [Blog] *Brookings Social Mobility Memos.* Available at: www.brookings.edu/blog/social-mobility-memos/2014/12/19/jingle-jangle-fallacies-for-non-cognitive-factors

4 Farrington, C.A., Roderick, M., Allensworth, E., Nagaoka, J., Keyes, T.S., Johnson, D.W., and Beechum, N.O. (2012). *Teaching Adolescents to Become Learners. The Role of Noncognitive Factors in Shaping School Performance: A Critical Literature Review.* Chicago: University of Chicago Consortium on Chicago School Research, p.2.

5 Reeves, R., Venator, J., and Howard, K. (2014). *The Character Factor: Measures and Impact of Drive and Prudence.* The Brookings Institution, p.4.

6 Williams, R. (2016). We Could Be Heroes. [Blog] *The New Statesman.* Available at: www.newstatesman.com/culture/books/2016/07/we-could-be-heroes-world-according-road-character

7 Gutman, L. and Schoon, I. (2013). *The Impact of Non-Cognitive Skills on Outcomes for Young People.* London: Institute of Education, Education Endowment Foundation, Cabinet Office, p.2.

8 Farrington, C.A., Roderick, M., Allensworth, E., Nagaoka, J., Keyes, T.S., Johnson, D.W., and Beechum, N.O. (2012). *Teaching Adolescents to Become Learners. The Role of Noncognitive Factors in Shaping School Performance: A Critical Literature Review.* Chicago: University of Chicago Consortium on Chicago School Research, p.9.

9 Dweck, C., Walton, G., and Cohen, G. (2011). *Academic Tenacity: Mindsets and Skills that Promote Long-Term Learning.* Seattle, WA: The Gates Foundation, p.4.

10 See note 7 above.

11 Duckworth, A. (2013). Grit and Self-Control [Online]. University of Pennsylvania Positive Psychology Center. Available at: www.authentichappiness.sas.upenn.edu/learn/grit

12 Hattie, J. and Yates, G. (2013). *Visible Learning and the Science of How We Learn.* Abingdon: Routledge, p.xvii.

13 Hattie, J. (2014). *Values-Led and Evidence-Informed Education—Exploring What Really Makes a Difference to Learning.* [Keynote Lecture to Whole Education's 5th Annual Conference]. London, 18 November 2014. Available at: https://visible-learning.org/2016/11/video-john-hatties-keynote-at-whole-education-conference

14 Gutman, L. and Schoon, I. (2013). *The Impact of Non-Cognitive Skills on Outcomes for Young People.* London: Institute of Education, Education Endowment Foundation, Cabinet Office, p.23.

15 Center on the Developing Child. (2015). *The Science of Resilience* (InBrief). Retrieved from www.developingchild.harvard.edu

16 See note 7 above.

17 Farrington, C.A., Roderick, M., Allensworth, E., Nagaoka, J., Keyes, T.S., Johnson, D.W., and Beechum, N.O. (2012). *Teaching Adolescents to Become Learners. The Role of Noncognitive Factors in Shaping School Performance: A Critical Literature Review.* Chicago: University of Chicago Consortium on Chicago School Research, p.7.

18 ibid. p.6.

19 See note 7 above.

2 Developing confidence, independence and resilience in the classroom

We've defined confidence, independence and resilience and attempted to map out the specific mindsets, habits and skills that pupils need, but how can teachers actually develop these things in the classroom? And how can they assess whether pupils are making progress? These are challenging questions, and the areas where there are currently the biggest gaps in the research. And yet, my team and I visited many teachers who appeared to be making an impact on their pupils' confidence, independence and resilience, and who were doing so deliberately and systematically. Before we explore what those teachers were doing, however, we should reflect briefly on two frequently asked questions:

- Can these mindsets and skills be explicitly taught? Don't they develop organically?
- Can their development really be integrated with academic learning?

Taught or caught

There's a reasonably common view that these kinds of outcomes develop organically in a positive, respectful classroom. 'I think it's all about relationships', one teacher said to me. 'I don't have any techniques or strategies as such.'

There's truth in this idea – classroom culture and positive relationships have a powerful effect on pupil confidence – but leaving things to chance is risky when working with large numbers of pupils and balancing multiple priorities. If your aim is to uproot and replace a range of unhelpful habits and mindsets, then a deliberate, structured approach has a far greater likelihood of success than generalised good intentions. Just as we wouldn't expect pupils to absorb key academic concepts by osmosis, this area also benefits from a plan with clear aims. It's often said of character and non-cognitive skills that they are 'caught not taught'. At the end of *Helping Children Succeed*, Paul Tough writes: 'Rather than consider noncognitive capacities as skills to be taught, I came to conclude, it's more accurate and useful to look at them as products of a child's environment.'[1] Again, there's sense in this remark – confidence isn't 'taught' in the way that algebra or the use of the semicolon would be – but there's a risk of this idea being misconstrued and leading teachers to infer that their influence on children's noncognitive capacities is therefore very limited. This is simply not the case. Through the way they teach and the way they set up their classroom, teachers are ideally placed to create the kind of conducive environment to which Tough is referring – a point that leads us directly into the next section about whether it's possible to integrate academic teaching and learning with the development of confidence, independence and resilience.

Doubling up

'You as their teacher are a scarce resource,' said Mark. 'There is only so much time and you end up making calls about what you can and can't do.' With so much material to cover, and so many competing demands, it can feel counter-intuitive to add yet more into the mix. Can a teacher really work on this area without stealing crucial time from academic learning?

This would certainly be an issue if a teacher used regular chunks of lesson time to work on these mindsets and skills in isolation, teaching 'resilience', for example, as though it were a stand-alone topic. However, a central tenet of this guide is that these non-academic outcomes can and should be pursued within and through academic work: through the way you set up your learning environment, and through the way you plan and structure your academic instruction, activities, discussions and routines. It does, of course, take some time to introduce and embed new concepts, routines and systems into the classroom. However, this investment is made with the faith that it will pay off across the year in the increased quality and intensity of pupils' work.

Academic study is challenging and, as such, it provides an ideal arena for working on confidence, independence and resilience. Over time the relationship between academic and non-academic outcomes becomes symbiotic, as the mindsets, skills and habits that pupils acquire make them increasingly capable at dealing with challenges and, consequently, accelerate their academic progress. Daniel Willingham describes the simple way that these distinct outcomes reinforce one another, stating that self-control, for example, 'predicts academic success because it makes you more likely to do the work to develop cognitive skills.'[2]

Coherent, logical, unmysterious

Having encountered teachers who were working deliberately on their pupils' confidence, independence and resilience, I studied their classrooms to try and understand what was happening and to see whether it was possible to extrapolate a replicable, sharable model from their practice. Early on it became apparent that there were similarities in approach between the teachers we visited, similarities that transcended phase, subject and school context, and that many of the techniques they were using were simple and transferable. I began extracting these common threads, mapping out what was happening and relating it to existing academic research.

The process of developing intangible-sounding skills and mindsets is sometimes viewed as challenging, elusive, even mysterious. In the process of assembling this model, however, I was struck by how coherent, logical and unmysterious it seemed. Essentially, the teachers I studied were approaching the development of confidence, independence and resilience with the same thought and care with which they approached academic learning: defining clear aims; making a plan and evaluating progress, creating a conducive classroom culture; and providing pupils with opportunities to build new habits and skills. They did a series of interconnected small things deliberately and systematically; as Doug Lemov said of the teachers he visited for his book *Teach Like a Champion,* they made 'a habit of small intentional habits, some of which might seem trivial,' but which they 'applied consistently and in coordination'[3].

Given the nature of the current debate about how character and non-cognitive skills develop – which often focuses on the value of trips, extra-curricular activities, or additional workshops – it was exciting to encounter teachers working on this area in the classroom day-to-day, without putting academic learning on hold to do so. Below is an attempt to codify and visualise what they were doing, in the hope that this model will support you to think through how to develop confidence, independence and resilience in your classroom. This approach consists of three distinct phases and types of teacher action:

1 **Knowing where you're going (p.36)**

   - Defining your aims for pupils, p.38
   - Translating your aims into a coherent plan, p.41
   - Establishing how you'll evaluate progress and feedback to pupils, p.43

2 **Creating the right conditions (p.48)**

   - Building trusting relationships and getting to know pupils, p.50
   - Providing ongoing encouragement, p.56

- Sharing and refining aims with pupils, p.61
- Ongoing discussion of pupils' aims and futures, p.65
- Establishing a classroom culture that welcomes risk taking and error, p.67

3   Building new habits (p.74)

- Supporting pupils:

  o   Enabling pupils to experience success and celebrating their progress, p.77

  o   Teaching pupils strategies to overcome challenges, p.83

  o   Enabling pupils to support, and seek support from, one another, p.89

- Challenging pupils

  o   Demanding maximum effort and quality from pupils, p.95

  o   Providing pupils with opportunities to work independently, p.102

  o   Expecting pupils to monitor and direct their own progress, p.106

The flowchart below (Figure 2.1) depicts this model and the relationship between the different phases. It is followed by two classroom case studies – one primary, one secondary - which bring this model to life and show the whole approach in action. In each case study you can observe a teacher setting bold aims, getting to know pupils and developing relationships, and establishing the routines and instruction that will enable them to address academic and non-academic outcomes simultaneously. The flowchart is necessarily rather neat and tidy; the case studies offer two different examples of how the different stages can look in practice and in combination in a busy classroom.

After the case studies you'll find the longest section of the book: a step-by-step guide to applying this model in your own classroom, breaking down each stage of the flowchart and giving practical examples and techniques.

Teacher actions flowchart

How to read this flowchart

This flowchart depicts the actions you need to take to develop your pupils' confidence, independence and resilience, deliberately and systematically. It is divided into the three phases discussed below:

1   Knowing where you're going
2   Creating the right conditions
3   Building new habits

In essence, the first phase is to do with planning and evaluation, the second with building relationships and creating a strong classroom culture, and the third with classroom instruction and routines.

The arrows looping back up to the 'Defining your aims for pupils' box indicate that this is an ongoing process, which evolves as you get to know your pupils, not something that happens once at the start of the year. The arrows looping back upwards from the 'Ongoing evaluation and feedback' box indicate that your evaluation informs the kind of support and challenge that you offer pupils.

Potential pitfalls

What gives this model its power is the fact that each step is part of a coherent approach. **This approach doesn't work if you miss steps out or only do bits of it.** The learning environment you create, and the experiences you provide for pupils, relate to the same aims and amplify one another, giving pupils multiple opportunities every lesson to develop new skills, mindsets and habits.

Some of the steps in this model may look unremarkable at first glance: building trusting relationships, for example, hardly sounds revolutionary, nor does encouraging pupils, celebrating progress or giving pupils the opportunity to work independently. Keep in mind, however, that many of **the familiar-seeming sections of this model need to be thought about and approached in a particular way, or accompanied by particular messages, for them to have an impact on your pupils' confidence, independence and resilience.** Although this model doesn't require you to reinvent the wheel, you may need to scrutinise and adapt elements of your existing practice.

As you explore each section of this guide you'll see that many of the practical ideas are quite simple, unflashy and not hugely time-consuming. These ideas are no less important for their simplicity and still need to be introduced and seen through effectively. **The key to using this approach well is consistency: ensuring that the dialogue, routines and teaching strategies you introduce are well embedded and regularly used.**

The reason that this book is structured around this teaching model, rather than simply offering a list of techniques, is because **confidence, independence and resilience are developed in the classroom through a deliberate, coherent, consistent approach, underpinned by regular monitoring and feedback.** Being structured and systematic allows your aims to filter down into

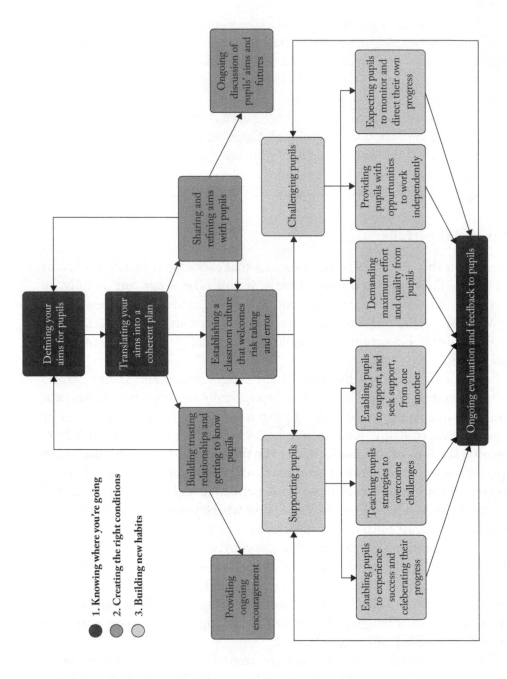

1. Knowing where you're going
2. Creating the right conditions
3. Building new habits

Figure 2.1 Teacher actions flowchart

every aspect of classroom life so that pupils are constantly practising the skills and mindsets that will make them act and feel confident, independent and resilient.

Habit-forming

The mindsets and skills that pupils need develop gradually, through repeated practice. Knowing about them in the abstract is not sufficient; they need to become the ways that pupils normally think and act.

It can be easy to overlook the fact that success and failure in classrooms hinges on what normally happens in them, minute by minute, lesson by lesson. As Graham Nuthall puts it, what pupils 'do in the classroom day after day is what they learn and become expert in.'[4] As such, 'normality' is a powerful force, legitimising, encouraging and perpetuating the attitudes and approach to learning in your classroom, for better or worse. And what normally happens in your classroom depends on your pupils' habits – the way they tend to think and act. This point came across powerfully in an interview I conducted with two of Lucy's maths pupils: 'At the start, it was *work hard, work hard, work hard, work hard*,' said Naomi, 'and now we've been working hard for so long, we don't even think about it anymore.' 'It's just the way it's become,' said Imogen. 'It's just the normal thing to do now in our class.'

Habits form in all classrooms, whether we plan for them or not. Harnessing this process – being deliberate about the habits that pupils form – is not difficult to do and can be exceedingly powerful, ensuring that the little things pupils do over and over again are meaningful and productive. This teaching model is, at base, about creating a certain kind of 'normal' environment in your classroom, built upon the habits of thought and action that will make pupils confident, independent, resilient learners.

The nineteenth century philosopher and psychologist, William James, was a passionate advocate for the power of habit in education:

> All our life, so far as it has definite form, is but a mass of habits, – practical, emotional, and intellectual, – systematically organized for our weal or woe, and bearing us irresistibly toward our destiny [. . .] [W]e are stereotyped creatures, imitators and copiers of our past selves. And since this, under any circumstances, is what we always tend to become, it follows first of all that the teacher's prime concern should be to ingrain into the pupil that assortment of habits that shall be most useful to him throughout life. Education is for behavior, and habits are the stuff of which behavior consists.[5]

His point that we are 'copiers of our past selves' is exactly what I heard from teachers, frustrated that pupils had inflexible ideas about themselves and their potential. In classrooms I saw teachers supporting pupils to break these ingrained patterns of behaviour and build the 'assortment of habits that shall be most useful to [them] throughout life.'

Another figure much quoted on the subject of habit is Aristotle. In *The Nicomachean Ethics* he argues that habits determine how we respond to situations and, ultimately, shape who we are. By 'being habituated to feel fear or confidence,' he says, 'we become brave or cowardly.'[6] It's hardly surprising, therefore, that Aristotle believed it was crucial to develop good habits from a young age: 'It makes no small difference, then, whether we form habits of one kind or of another from our very youth; it makes a very great difference, or rather all the difference.'[7]

What is sometimes absent in discussions of Aristotle's thoughts on habit is a sense of how deliberate we need to be to form them. In her introduction to *The Nicomachean Ethics*, Oxford philosophy professor Lesley Brown writes that Aristotle's approach to habit formation 'is not to be thought of as unthinking, but rather as intentional habituation, which then becomes second nature.'[8] This idea of 'intentional habituation' is central to the approach outlined in this guide and something you'll encounter in the case studies in the coming pages: teachers defining the habits their pupils need and introducing routines and strategies that give them the opportunity to practise new ways of thinking and acting until they become automatic.

Notes

1 Tough, P. (2016). *Helping Children Succeed: What Works and Why*. 1st ed. [PDF], p.18.
2 Willingham, D. (2013). How Children Succeed. [Blog] Daniel Willingham: Science and Education Blog. Available at: www.danielwillingham.com/daniel-willingham-science-and-education-blog/how-children-succeed
3 Lemov, D. (2015). *Teach Like a Champion 2.0*. San Francisco: Jossey-Bass, p.24.
4 Nuthall, G. (2007). *The Hidden Lives of Learners*. Wellington, New Zealand: NZCER Press, p.36.
5 James, W. (1899). *Talks to Teachers on Psychology: And to Students on Some of Life's Ideals*. New York: Henry Holt and Company, p.66.
6 Aristotle. (2009). *The Nicomachean Ethics*. Oxford: Oxford University Press, p.24.
7 ibid.
8 Brown, L. (2009). Endnote. In: Aristotle, ed., *The Nicomachean Ethics*. Oxford: Oxford University Press, p.212.

3 Case study
Lian, year 2

At the start of the year, many of Lian's pupils were very reliant on adult support, anxious about making mistakes and uncomfortable attempting challenging work. 'My vision was that they would feel invincible about learning', says Lian. 'That if they put their mind to it, and if they practise the skills that we teach them, they would be able to learn whatever they want.' Specifically, she says, she wanted her Year 2 pupils 'to be motivated', 'to be highly skilled learners', and to 'learn to challenge themselves and enjoy challenge'.

The day-to-day details of the classroom flow directly from these overarching aims: Lian weaves strategies for developing key mindsets, skills and habits into her class routines, her instruction and her interactions with pupils. Rather than 'explicitly teaching these skills,' she told me, 'they were all embedded into their normal lessons. I wanted to equip pupils to be able to learn but didn't isolate the skills and teach them as a subject. I taught them as they learnt the curriculum.'

Carole and Gabriella, the two teaching assistants working with Lian, were struck by the focus and determination with which Lian targeted these outcomes: 'One thing I've never seen in a teacher is how much she pushes their learning skills,' said Carole. 'She's not really about achieving – obviously she is, she's a teacher – but it's not all achievement based. It's all about progression: she celebrates progression and she celebrates mistakes and it's all about the steps to get there.' Gabriella stressed that Lian's central aim is for her pupils to be 'independent, really. Not just in their work, but independent in every other aspect of their lives as well.'

Explicitly discussing pupils' aims and learning with them

At the start of the year, Lian shared her aims with pupils and talked about their learning in a whole-class discussion. 'Who's responsible for your learning?' she asked them. 'They all pointed at me, and I was like, *Nope – I'm not responsible for your learning, I'm responsible for teaching. You're responsible for your learning.* And you just saw this light bulb kind of turn on.'

After that initial conversation, independence became an ongoing theme in Lian's classroom, something that she and her teaching assistants mention on a daily basis. 'She constantly pushes their independence,' Carole says, 'and the fact that *if I want to learn something, it's my job to learn it, not the teacher's job.*'

Ensuring children are ready to start the day

Lian and her teaching assistants give a couple of children who display a lot of attention-seeking behaviour a 'five minute one-to-one intensive' at the start of the day. 'They have five minutes with one of the adults to chat to them and ask them how they are, to calm them down and get them ready to start the day.' Ensuring pupils are in the right state of mind avoids 'having to deal with behaviour' later on.

Celebrating mistakes as opportunities for learning

'We talk about mistakes, how it's fine to make mistakes,' says Lian. 'We celebrate mistakes: we have a thing called, "Best Mistake of the Day" for the mistake we can learn the most from. They do it better than me now; they'll notice someone else's mistake and they're like, *Oh, that could be the best mistake of the day!*'

Seeing mistake making as part of learning makes her pupils more comfortable taking risks and more likely to persevere when they find something challenging. Lian makes a note of the best mistake each day in the corner of her class whiteboard.

Making the steps to success visible to pupils

When pupils begin a complex task, Lian writes the steps they need to take on a large laminated yellow staircase. 'The Steps-to-Success are really useful', according to Gabriella, 'because they can be for anything and the child can actually see what they have to do'. Children who might otherwise think '*Well I don't know what to do now, so I'm just going to sit here and not do it*' are now able to navigate a new piece of work without additional adult input. The-Steps-to-Success show pupils what's required to complete a given task and act as a stepping stone to working independently.

Lian also created Steps-to-Success for a few essential, recurring tasks (answering reading comprehension questions, for example, and solving the four basic maths operations) and taught her children to memorise them so that they also have a system for completing these important, commonplace activities.

Teaching children to support one another

'A lot of them, if there was something they didn't really know, they would just say *I'm stuck*', Lian says, thinking back to the start of the year. Furthermore, 'they wouldn't say what they were stuck on.' As such, she wanted them to have strategies for dealing with being stuck: 'to be able to find what they're stuck on' and also 'to be able to ask the question that's going to help them find the answer.'

She introduced 'learning partners' so that pupils could become more of a support for one another and practise these skills together. 'If you're stuck, you ask your learning partner,' says one pupil, 'and if your learning partner is stuck with you, you ask the teacher instead.' Teaching pupils to support each other effectively wasn't straightforward. At first, pupils didn't know how to work well with one another and weren't making the most of their time in pairs. 'I realised it was because I hadn't told them what to do,' says Lian. 'Well, I might have told them in September what I wanted to do, but they didn't have a constant reminder of that.'

As such Lian:

- Models effective partner work with her teaching assistants, talking aloud so that pupils know exactly what's required and have an example to follow.
- Displays visual aids: photos of learning partners working effectively together.
- Points out and praises good learning partner work, noting the best learning partners each day on the board.

As the routine has become more firmly embedded, Lian has mixed learning partners up so that pupils get used to working well with anybody in the class, not just their friends. 'At first we picked the learning partners', Carole said, 'now we just pull them out of a hat.'

Setting up these learning partners both decreases pupil dependence on adults and develops a spirit of mutual endeavour among classmates. Pupils now know that they need to help themselves and each other first of all. 'She helps us if we're really, really stuck', said one pupil about Lian.

Visualising and celebrating pupil progress

'They think they're in blue and they want to be in orange,' says one of Lian's teaching assistants, 'that they *can* be in orange, they *can* progress.' One of the ways that Lian shows pupils the progress they're making in literacy is on a train displayed on the wall. The carriages correspond to different academic levels and every half term, after a literacy assessment, pupils move a photograph of themselves to the appropriate point further along the train. This means that not only the adults 'know their progress, they know their progress'.

Explaining the system, one pupil said: 'We start on this [carriage] and then we move up every half term until we get to here – but as you can see, Kelly and Jack have moved past the cloud [of steam at the front of the railway engine].'

Showing the whole class advancing in their learning embeds the notion that everyone can learn and achieve and celebrates improvement over absolute results. 'We consistently value progress over attainment,' says Lian, 'so they value that somebody has learned something and made progress rather than someone has got a high mark.' Doing this was a way to develop a 'growth mindset', the belief 'that they could grow their intelligence.'

Keeping targets present day-to-day and enabling pupils to monitor their progress

Once pupils have moved their photos along the train and set themselves a new target, each individual is given a 'Magic List': two or three bullet points outlining the next steps they need to take in their writing. 'I got the children to memorise them', says Lian, 'and then jot them down at the top of every piece of writing they did in class. It meant they were more likely to write pieces that met all the necessary criteria.' Once pupils understand and remember the areas they need to work on next, they can assess their own literacy work, checking that they've included the required features. This hands pupils more responsibility for their progress than they might feel otherwise. 'I don't know any other 6-year olds', says Carole, 'that can sit and self-assess their own work and go *Oh, I forgot a conjunction, I forgot my capital letters and full stops.*'

Using precise, advanced language with pupils

Challenging pupils with academically advanced material is another way to demonstrate high expectations of pupils and can be a boost to children's confidence and self-belief. 'Over the last two days we investigated the organisational features and language features of a non-chronological report', Lian says to her class at the start of a lesson. She could translate that sentence into simpler terms; instead, she introduces her pupils to terms that will be useful to them later. She then invests time in explaining them. Many challenging terms or concepts recur across the year and pass into the common vocabulary of the class.

Allowing pupils to select and adjust the difficulty level of their work

Sometimes Lian sets several different challenges at different levels and if pupils 'start on a challenge and they're finding it easy, they can move on to a more difficult one to challenge themselves'. Lian's aim is for pupils to take more ownership of their learning and to independently opt for more and more challenging work, to 'want to challenge themselves and find that satisfying'. 'I don't let them have complete free reign in this', Lian clarifies; she would step in if they selected a task that was clearly inappropriate.

In conclusion . . . Lian's pupils not only got excellent Year 2 SATs results, they also made significant strides in the way they thought about and approached their learning. 'Because of her pushing the challenges,' says one teaching assistant, 'and pushing their independence and pushing them to *You do it, you do it, you do it*, now I'd say at the end of the year, some children who would cry if they found anything hard are now like *Yeah, I'll do it*.'

Relating this case study to the model on p.20

How do Lian's aims relate to the aims on the outcomes flowchart (p.6) and success criteria (pp.7–10) in this guide?

How, and how far, can you see her aims playing out in her classroom practice?

What role do evaluation and feedback play in Lian's attempts to meet her aims?

What does Lian do to build relationships and create a classroom culture conducive to developing confidence, independence and resilience?

Which of Lian's actions are focused on supporting her pupils? How far do they correspond with the three types of support outlined on the flowchart?

Which of Lian's actions are focused on challenging her pupils? How far do they correspond with the three types of challenge outlined on the flowchart?

To what extent do academic and non-academic aims seem to be integrated in this classroom?

4 Case study

Kayleigh, year 9 French

When I visit, Kayleigh's school is failing and about to close down. Her pupils are well aware of this, Kayleigh tells me, and this damages 'their perception of themselves and what they think they are able to do in life and in the classroom.' As such, Kayleigh is determined to make her pupils 'realise that they are capable of things that they considered to be impossible.' 'They have very low self-esteem', she says, and many of them look at French and think: '*I can't do that, I'm not clever enough, I'm not smart enough for that.*' Precisely because her pupils see modern languages as difficult, Kayleigh sees her subject as a 'good tool' for challenging fixed mindsets and showing her pupils that 'through hard work and perseverance and enthusiasm you can do it'. 'I want them to be people who recognise the capacity for growth within themselves', she says, and she treats the academic study of French as a medium for developing mindsets, skills and habits that will help them succeed in her classroom and beyond. 'Although these are skills that they are developing in a slow way and on a small-scale,' she says, 'they're skills that they can apply elsewhere.' She turns persevering with French into a broader lesson about perseverance; gaining confidence in French into a broader sense of confidence.

All the details of Kayleigh's classroom – the way she talks to pupils, the activities she plans, her class routines, resources and displays – are part of a holistic effort to develop her pupils' confidence, independence and resilience. Crucially, though, they are the same strategies she uses to support academic success; Kayleigh pursues non-academic ends through academic means, adapting aspects of her French teaching so that she addresses both areas simultaneously.

I visited Kayleigh's Year 9 French class, who she'd been teaching since the start of Year 8. They had had 'quite a negative experience' with French in Year 7, she told me, and 'were not enthusiastic' when she first met them. 'It was: *Who are you? We don't know you.* So my first challenge was to gain their trust ... It wasn't a rapid thing.' 'When I was in Year 8', one of Kayleigh's pupils told me, 'I thought foreign languages were really hard and I used to overreact and say *Oh my god, I can't do this, I can't do that*. You know? Overreact.'

Discussing pupils' short and long term aims

Kayleigh peppers her lessons with conversations – whether in English or in French – about what pupils want to do when they're older and why. In tandem, she challenges fixed mindsets, asking questions like: 'Why do you think that? Why can't you go to university? What's stopping you?' and encouraging them to think through challenges constructively: 'What knowledge do you need? What skills do you need? What support do you need to get you there?'

'I don't have the skills to help them become a doctor,' she says, 'but what I can do is help them develop the belief in themselves, and teach them how to have aims, set goals, and persevere and achieve them.' Maintaining a constant conversation about the 'skills that they are going to need later on in life to achieve their aspirations' is itself a crucial part of fostering them; by making these skills explicit day-to-day, pupils are better able to understand them and take ownership of developing them.

Consulting pupils on what they enjoy and find helpful in lessons

As well as being a good way to get to know pupils, build relationships and inform lesson planning, asking pupils about what they enjoy doing in lessons and what has helped them learn in the past is a way of respecting them and making them feel like they are being taken seriously. 'At the start of the year she asked us what we want in our lessons', one of Kayleigh's pupils told me, 'and she gave us a piece of paper and everybody wrote what they wanted. Most of the people put games, key words and pieces of writing, and she put everything together and made the lessons.' Although Kayleigh ultimately decides how to plan her lessons most effectively, she consults her pupils and gives them a voice in this process.

Giving specific praise, focused on progress

Kayleigh makes a point of praising effort and progress – the 'fact that they have gone for it and really tried' – rather than praising absolute attainment. But she believes that effective praise isn't just a matter of 'saying *Oh well done that's brilliant*, but also saying why what they have done was good … making them aware of the intricacies of what they need to do to achieve.' Praising pupils' progress supports the development of a growth mindset, reinforcing the message that, with effort, they can be successful. It incentivises pupils to try even harder; Kayleigh describes this as giving pupils 'the confidence to be more confident'.

Asking pupils to consider why they're doing what they're doing

Kayleigh frequently asks her pupils, 'What is the purpose of doing this activity? Why are we doing it?' Having this conversation ensures that they are consciously focusing on the desired outcomes for each piece of work and getting the maximum benefit from it.

'Are there are any other skills we're developing whilst we're doing this whiteboard activity?' Kayleigh asked her pupils when I visited. 'Spontaneous writing', said one. 'Confidence,' said another. In reply, Kayleigh nodded and said: 'We should have the confidence to walk into the writing exam and think, *Yeah, I can write in French.* And by practising like this with a pen on a whiteboard, you're gaining that confidence and you're gaining those skills.'

Allowing pupils to monitor their progress by making success criteria explicit

Giving pupils access to detailed success criteria, and teaching them how to use them effectively, demystifies how to succeed at a complex task. It allows pupils to independently monitor their progress and to take ownership of their development. 'There is a very clear structure to help them see how to get to each grade, and what they need to do to improve', says Kayleigh. 'Something I have really focused on with this class is making them incredibly aware of the criteria for success. That's allowed them to become very independent.'

Pupils have the mark scheme stuck into the back of their books. When Kayleigh marks their work, she uses the scoring system from the mark scheme so that they can see exactly what they've done well and what they need to do to improve. Her pupils are now used to consulting the mark scheme and working out their next steps. 'You score points for each thing that you do', says William, 'you get 15 points for communication and you can get up to 10 points for your language and 5 points for your accuracy. You need 17 points for a C and, if you get something like 16, you look in the back of your book and it will tell you how you get the 17 to get your C. It tells you the next step to do.'

Letting pupils choose the difficulty level of their work

'In some of the activities that I do,' says Kayleigh, 'I give the pupils a choice: *Do you want to start on a red task, orange task, or a green task?* And some of them will start on the red task but, by the end, they gain that little bit of confidence and that little bit of self-belief to have a go at the green one.' Kayleigh pushes pupils to move from the easiest activities and challenge themselves, but leaves the choice and the timing down to them. 'If you started on the red activity like Ray did,' she said to the class on my visit, 'Ray has already, without me even asking him to, moved down and he's now giving reasons and opinions. So if you think you're being safe and just sticking to the red activity, try and push yourself.'

Her pupils commented on the way that work is structured to allow them to move seamlessly from accessible to challenging work. 'We begin easy', said one pupil, 'and then we make it slightly harder and harder, so we are actually working hard and trying our best.' 'She gives us hard work in an easy way', said another, 'it's hard, but she gives it in an easy way.'

Teaching pupils to set their own targets

After pupils have looked at a piece of marked work, they set themselves three targets, which they consult during their next independent task. 'Now I don't even have to tell them that *You need to set yourself three targets based on what I have written about your work*', says Kayleigh. 'They will set about doing that independently and they will refer back to those the next time that they come to do a piece of writing.'

By expecting pupils to set targets, Kayleigh ensures that they learn as much as possible from every piece of work and understand how they'll improve next time around. This maximises the value of each piece of work as an opportunity to build confidence and independence: pupils become increasingly confident as they notice and reflect on their successes, and they become more independent by taking charge of their own progression. Kayleigh reinforces this process with short bursts of whole-class discussion about target setting, asking 'Who can tell me what they're going to improve for next time?' and sharing examples of pupils who have met their own targets. 'Last lesson William said *I am going to write 25 lines*', Kayleigh tells the class, 'and he worked at that for the whole lesson and he achieved it. I was really impressed with him because he set himself a target, he stuck to it and got there, and he got a really good grade because of it.'

Using displays to celebrate progress and encourage pupils to learn from one another

Kayleigh displays pupil writing on her classroom walls. She chooses pieces that exemplify a specific feature that pupils need to include in their GCSE French writing, labelling each piece so that pupils know what to look for and learn from. 'Aalia has really got her head around how to structure her paragraphs,' said Kayleigh to her class, 'and what I've done is I've photocopied that piece of work and it's up on the wall. It says next to it: *Do you know how to structure a paragraph as well as Aalia?* So if you want to see a really well structured piece of work, go and have a look at it.'

This display functions as a tangible correlate to the mark scheme glued into pupils' books, and encourages them to match their own areas for development with the learning opportunities provided by the work of their peers. 'With our display board it's about saying: *Jamal's really good at this, go and look at what Jamal's done, go and look at Huan's work, she's really good at using the past tense*', Kayleigh explains. Her displays allow her to 'highlight the key skills that each person brings to the table', with each pupil from across 'a vast ability range' celebrated as an example of success that their peers can learn from.

Making resources available so that pupils can solve their own problems

'Miss always makes a new learning mat for every subject', James told me. 'We use learning mats when we are doing our writing.' Kayleigh's learning mats feature the key vocabulary for a new topic, along with any new linguistic constructions they're learning. The mats are available during independent work and each pupil can decide when, how and how much to use it. As well as the topic-specific mats, in the corner of the classroom is a shelf of dictionaries, which pupils are welcome to consult when they want. Nearby, assorted laminated resource sheets hang off hooks on the wall. To get pupils into the habit of finding the information they need to solve their problems, Kayleigh regularly reminds them that resources are available but doesn't dictate when to use them.

Encouraging pupils to consult one another when they're struggling

Kayleigh wants her pupils to view one another as a source of knowledge and support in the classroom. As such, when they're struggling at a piece of work, they're expected to consult three of their peers before coming to her. 'We have to ask three people about a word or something before we go and ask the teacher', explained one of her pupils.

Asking pupils to give one another verbal feedback

'I'm looking for my angels and my demons', said Kayleigh after a pupil has read out a piece of work in French. Pupils volunteer as angels, identifying what went well, or demons, identifying areas for improvement.

'She used high quality phrases', said an angel.

'Can we be more specific about what she included?' Kayleigh asked. 'Jamal, do you want to be an angel?'

'She added someone else's opinion in there,' he replied, 'she said why her Mum likes dancing.'

'I'm going to have to ask what the demons think now', Kayleigh said. 'They're very eager today.' 'I didn't like the pace', said a demon. 'It could have been a bit slower.'

Kayleigh is constantly asking her pupils to evaluate one another's work, sometimes through routines like Angels and Demons – a light-hearted way for pupils to get used to offering frank, critical feedback on their peers' work – and sometimes as part of other tasks. 'I want you to discuss the good things about each answer', Kayleigh said after pupils had completed a short written task. 'So Ray is going to tell Luke what's good about his answer, Jamal is going to tell Brian what's good about his answer – then you're going to compare.' These kinds of conversations contribute to a trusting culture in which it's fine to make mistakes and everyone supports everyone else to improve.

Teaching pupils to mark one another's work and write comments

As well as asking pupils to give one another verbal feedback, Kayleigh provides them with more in-depth opportunities to critique their classmates' work and offer written feedback; looking at work by classmates provides a mirror for their own.

'We do a lot of peer assessment', Kayleigh says, 'and every time we do a piece of writing I get them to mark each other's work. The feedback that they write in each other's books now is so thoughtful: *You could use this sentence because this means this* or *Why not put this in here?* They actually really want to help each other.'

Asking pupils to mark their peers' work treats them as experts for one another, able to support their peers to succeed, and affirms their sense that they understand what's required to be successful. 'We have peer markers as well telling us what we need to do', says Jamal. 'You can ask anyone to say what you've done well, what your weakness is and what your next step is', says Sarah.

Encouraging inter-class, not intra-class, competition

'Just before Christmas I had a really big challenge', says Kayleigh. 'The classroom started to be really competitive, so when they got their marks back they would say *I got an 18* or *I got a 16* and they were almost getting quite nasty with it.' To harness this competitive spirit and snuff out antagonism between classmates, Kayleigh launched an inter-class competition, pitting two French classes against one another. At the end of each week she adds up all of the pupils' results to get a class average. She then plots both results onto a wall chart so that pupils can see how their class is doing as a whole. 'I have been able to use that', she explains, 'to say, *Well, if you want our class average to be better than the other class you need to be helping each other more.*'

Kayleigh frequently refers to this competition in lessons. 'The average grade for this class now is 17. And who can tell me what grade that is? A C! On average as a class you're getting a C – that is so impressive, especially when you're still in year 9 ... This class is rocketing up the competition board, because you're so good at helping each other.'

In conclusion ... Initially pupils thought '*We'll never be able to speak French, we'll never be able to write an essay like* that', Kayleigh told me. 'Now, they *can* do it. They are now proud of themselves because they have done something that they thought wasn't possible.' 'All the confidence we have, we are not just going to lose it', said her pupil Sarah, when I asked how she felt about having to move elsewhere when the school closes down. 'We are going to use that confidence and instead of needing the teacher to encourage us, we should just encourage ourselves.'

Relating this case study to the model on p.20

How do Kayleigh's aims relate to the aims on the outcomes flowchart (p.6) and success criteria (pp.7–10) in this guide?

How, and how far, can you see her aims playing out in her classroom practice?

What role do evaluation and feedback play in Kayleigh's attempts to meet her aims?

What does Kayleigh do to build relationships and create a classroom culture conducive to developing confidence, independence and resilience?

Which of Kayleigh's actions are focused on supporting her pupils? How far do they correspond with the three types of support outlined on the flowchart?

Which of Kayleigh's actions are focused on challenging her pupils? How far do they correspond with the three types of challenge outlined on the flowchart?

To what extent do academic and non-academic aims seem to be integrated in this classroom?

5 Knowing where you're going

The first step in developing pupils' confidence, independence and resilience is deciding to do it at all. Simple as this may sound, it's a critical step; unless you deliberately commit to working on this area and outline clear aims, all you have are good intentions.

The process of setting ambitious aims for pupils' growth in confidence, independence and resilience, and using them to inform your planning, is similar to the process of setting ambitious academic goals, planning backwards from them, and mapping out learning across the year. As with academic learning, these outcomes benefit from a structured, carefully thought-out approach – a point made in the 'Building Blocks for Learning' report:

> It is well understood that students build academic skills through effective modelling, scaffolding (or support) and opportunities to apply and transfer them independently. It is also well understood that students must develop foundational academic skills before higher-order skills. Children's behavioural, social, emotional and cognitive development requires this same design, attention and support.[1]

On a long sea journey, surrounded by a featureless expanse, knowing where you're going and tracking progress towards your destination is the thing that gets you there. Likewise in the classroom, knowing the impact you want to have on pupils, and how you'll know what progress they're making, is a critical part of making that impact at all. The thinking and planning you do before setting out is the groundwork for everything that follows.

Defining your aims for pupils

- Aim to make a significant impact on pupils' confidence, independence and resilience
- Break your overarching aims down into smaller, tangible goals with clear success criteria

Translating your aims into a coherent plan

- Plan backwards from your overarching aims and map out smaller goals across the year
- Plan out the learning environment and experiences that will enable pupils to meet your goals

Establishing how you'll evaluate progress and feedback to pupils

- Decide how and when you'll gather information on pupil progress
- Use the information you gather to adjust your plan as required

Defining your aims for pupils

- **Aim to make a significant impact on pupils' confidence, independence and resilience**
- **Break your overarching aims down into smaller, tangible goals with clear success criteria**

One of the challenges of working with pupils who are struggling or very far behind is defining what it means to have high expectations for them. Should you relativise your expectations, academic or otherwise, according to the context? I once attended an event on this subject and heard a range of similar questions:

- 'How do you marry ambitious aims with the limits of your situation?'
- 'When pupils are so far behind, isn't a low grade a genuinely good achievement?'
- 'How do you make pupils believe they can do what they want with their lives without crushing them under crippling expectations?'

These are understandable questions, especially when teachers find themselves approaching major national tests with pupils who are a long way from meeting even the most basic expectations. And yet, as another teacher at the same event said, young people 'don't get to write *I got an E, but I went to a struggling school* on their university application.' When we dilute our expectations for young people we confirm and perpetuate a cycle of low confidence and under-achievement. The very fact of being uncompromising and aiming for challenging, improbable goals, can itself be the catalyst for reversing negative trends, enabling pupils to surprise themselves, and building the confidence, independence and resilience that propels them to levels of success they might never have contemplated.

Aim to make a significant impact on pupils' confidence, independence and resilience

A classroom's overarching aims should transform what takes place there, informing even the smallest decisions and allowing the teacher to steer a course through competing pressures and priorities.

The claim of this book is that, alongside highly ambitious academic aims, teachers should explicitly aim to ensure that all of their pupils become confident, independent, resilient learners. These two types of aim are intimately connected, as outlined on p.xxi: confidence, independence and resilience underpin and accelerate academic success, and a lack of them can be a major barrier to achievement.

Each of these three qualities is an essential support for the others. When Nicole told me that her objective was 'to encourage and support independence', she immediately added that 'this obviously also involves building up confidence and resilience' so that her pupils are 'able to, and want to, become independent.' When Lian says she wants her pupils to feel 'invincible about learning' (see p.23), when Kayleigh says she wants her pupils to 'realise that they are capable of things that they considered to be impossible' (see p.28), and when Dan says he wants his pupils 'not to feel at all inhibited by anything' (see p.xi), they're all describing outcomes that require confidence *and* independence *and* resilience: changes to the way that pupils view themselves, their learning and their future, and to the skills and habits that enable them to affect each of those domains.

Few teachers would say, if questioned, that they didn't want their pupils to have the confidence, independence and resilience to make great academic progress. It's different, however, to make this an explicit aim and to pursue it relentlessly and systematically with your pupils. Doing so guides your planning, informs your decision making and shapes even the most incidental details of your classroom.

Break your overarching aims down into smaller, tangible goals with clear success criteria

Unless you unpack your aims and break them into smaller, more specific goals, saying that you want pupils to become confident, independent and resilient risks being little more than an expression of good will. To give your aims real meaning and force, you need to:

- Get to know pupils and gather information on their strengths and areas for development at the start of the year
- Define the specific skills and mindsets that pupils will need to acquire in order to achieve your overarching aims for them
- Consider how these skills and mindsets relate to one another and the order in which pupils need to develop

The heart of this book is the flowchart of outcomes and list of accompanying success criteria on pp.6–10. This is an attempt to plot out the specific skills and mindsets that, together, make pupils act and feel confident, independent and resilient. Its principle aim is to support you with the goal setting and evaluation process. Specifically, you can use this outcomes flowchart:

- **Diagnostically**, to support you to establish where your pupils are at the start of the year
- **To guide your planning**, using it as a route map through the various skills and mindsets pupils need. The table shows how these outcomes seem to interrelate and suggests the sequence in which you should work on them
- **To support evaluation**, using the statements beneath each mindset and skill as simple success criteria
- **To provide a common language** for discussing this area with your pupils, ensuring that terms are understood and being used in the same way by all

Coming up with a sequence of clear, tangible goals is essential for your planning. The benefits of this process are further amplified when you share these goals with your pupils (see p.61). As Dweck, Cohen and Walton write: 'the simple act of breaking long-term lofty goals into concrete and short-term steps promotes student learning and motivation'[2]. Showing your pupils the staging posts on the way to success helps them to believe that success is possible and take greater responsibility for bringing it about.

Translating your aims into a coherent plan

- **Plan backwards from your overarching aims and map out smaller goals across the year**
- **Plan out the learning environment and experiences that will enable pupils to meet your goals**

Lian describes how thinking carefully about her aims 'was important to help me understand what I want for these kids' but that 'then I had to decide how was that going to impact my classroom practice *now*'. To be meaningful and effective, your macro-level aims for pupils need to be apparent in the micro-level details of the classroom lesson to lesson. And for that to happen, you need to translate your aims into a coherent plan.

Plan backwards from your overarching aims and map out smaller goals across the year

When planning for academic progress you would begin with your end of year aims and plan backwards, mapping out the content to be taught and intermediate milestones to hit at different points. You can follow the same process for developing confidence, independence and resilience:

- Begin with a clear list of the specific mindsets, skills and habits that you want pupils to have acquired by the end of the year
- Plot out the moments in the year by which you want pupils to have acquired them
- Map out when you'll need to begin working on particular outcomes in order to hit those milestones

Building your pupils' confidence, independence and resilience involves, for the most part, developing and embedding habits of thought and action and, as such, a lot of your activity will be front-loaded and integrated with the classroom relationships, dialogue, routines and systems that you introduce at the start of the year and maintain throughout. There will, however, be certain skills and mindsets that require specific experiences or opportunities, and others that need to be introduced later in the year once you've laid the foundations for them.

Plan out the learning environment and experiences that will enable pupils to meet your goals

Once you have a plan for the year, outlining what you're trying to achieve and when, you can begin to assemble the learning environment and experiences that will enable your pupils to advance towards your goals. Again, because developing confidence, independence and resilience involves working on mindsets and building new habits, all aspects of classroom life – relationships, dialogue, routines, culture, systems, instruction – have the potential to be influential. Pupils need to be immersed in an environment that fosters new ways of thinking and acting, and given experiences that allow them to practise and strengthen them.

Much of the rest of this book is about how to create that environment and give pupils those experiences. The next section, 'Creating the right conditions' (from p.46), is about how to set up a powerful environment through your classroom culture, dialogue and relationships. The section that follows, 'Building new habits' (from p.71), is about giving pupils the resources, skills and experiences they need to develop and practise new ways of thinking and behaving.

Although this guide contains lots of practical ideas that you can adopt or adapt, it isn't an exhaustive list and I hope that the cumulative effect of exploring the tactics and techniques mentioned here is that you feel equipped to make up new ones of your own.

Establishing how you'll evaluate progress and feedback to pupils

- **Decide how and when you'll gather information on pupil progress**
- **Use the information you gather to adjust your plan as required**

You have aims and a plan; the final part of this phase is establishing how you'll evaluate pupils' developing confidence, independence and resilience and give them feedback on their progress. It's essential to decide this in advance so that evaluation and feedback can be embedded into the process of *making impact* and not simply used to *assess impact* after the fact.

In the classroom, evaluation – whether of academic progress or other mindsets and skills – isn't merely a way to understand your impact, it's also one of the most powerful levers for making an impact in the first place. Good evaluation enables you to track progress and change tack if required; likewise, good feedback is among the most powerful tools for learning and motivation at your disposal, showing pupils their successes, showing them how to improve, and increasing their agency and sense of ownership. A significant amount of the approach outlined here operates *through* the feedback process: the moments at which pupils learn how they're progressing and, based on what they discover, make a decision about what they'll do next and how much effort they'll invest in it.

The EEF's Teaching and Learning Toolkit identifies feedback as one of the two most powerful mechanisms for accelerating pupil progress.[3] Dylan Wiliam describes it as 'perhaps the central process in effective instruction'[4] and John Hattie writes that the act of constantly 'seeking evidence relating to the three feedback questions ("Where am I going?'; 'How am I going there?'; 'Where to next?"') [. . .] is among the most powerful influences on student achievement that we know.'[5] This was a message I heard from pupils too. 'When we have good feedback,' one pupil told me, 'we know what to do: what's wrong and how to improve it.'

Wiliam also makes the important point that the EEF toolkit provides an aggregate score based on how interventions *have tended to be used*, rather than offering an objective evaluation of their potential to make an impact on students.[6] Powerful as assessment can be, feedback cannot be approached unthinkingly. As John Hattie writes, effective assessment is not simply a technical process, it's also about 'how teachers think about themselves'. In Hattie's view, teachers need to see themselves 'as evaluators of their impact, and as change agents purposely setting up conditions to impact on learning.'[7]

Decide how and when you'll gather information on pupil progress

Evaluating progress in intangible-seeming mindsets and skills is more challenging than assessing academic progress: apart from certain surveys that measure particular attributes, there isn't an accepted way to evaluate impact in this area. Saying that, there are various ways to proceed in the absence of robust tools and tests. Here are three approaches to consider and, perhaps, combine:

1   **Monitoring visible changes in what pupils say and do**

As confidence, independence and resilience have a major impact on the way that pupils talk about and approach their learning, the simplest way of tracking their growth is observation – a technique that Early Years practitioners use to assess their pupils (see p.115). You can watch for changes in:

- The quality and quantity of pupil's work, in class and at home
- The amount of time on task
- The habits and strategies that pupils employ in class
- The way pupils talk about themselves and their learning
- The way pupils react to error and challenging work

The success criteria below each mindset or skill on the outcomes table (see pp.6–10) provide a useful starting point for thinking about the things you might see and hear from pupils that would give you confidence that they are developing in these areas. For example, if you're trying to develop persistence you'd be looking for evidence of the following:

- I keep going when I'm struggling
- I select and apply strategies to help myself
- I find the resources I need
- I only ask the teacher for help when I've exhausted all other options
- I complete pieces of independent work
- I practise to get better at things

These are tangible, observable outcomes that you can monitor in the classroom. Whether you formally track them, or are simply aware of and alert to them while you're teaching, will depend very much on how many pupils you work with. Primary teachers could have a sheet of relevant statements printed out for each pupil and tick them off over the course of the year once they seem secure. For secondary teachers, teaching multiple classes, this is likely to be unfeasible; as an alternative, you could run occasional whole-class sessions in which you show pupils these lists of outcomes and give them the opportunity to reflect on their own progress in this area.

The advantage of focusing on observable changes to behaviour is that 'virtually all other noncognitive factors work through academic behaviors to affect performance', as the University of Chicago review puts it.[8] The way a pupil approaches their work is a concrete manifestation of how they feel about it, how they feel about themselves, and the skills they possess to tackle it. And 'because they are observable behaviors,' the Chicago review continues, 'they are also relatively easy to describe, monitor, and measure.'[9]

2 Using pupils' attendance and grades as proxy measures

Daniel Willingham suggests that basic measures of pupils' school attendance and academic performance can be taken as meaningful proxies for the development of other mindsets and skills. He gives the example of trying to evaluate whether pupils have become more resilient in the absence of a 'psychometrically sound measure of resilience':

> My real interest is student outcomes like grades, attendance, dropout, completion of assignments, class participation and so on. There is no reason not to measure these as my outcome variables.

Willingham's point is that these are the kinds of outcomes we're hoping that resilience will enable pupils to achieve. Although they're affected by too many factors for us to say exactly what role resilience played, at least, he continues, 'I'm measuring the outcome I actually care about'.[10] This isn't to imply that confidence, independence and resilience aren't valuable in their own right, simply that they're difficult to measure and looking at other outcomes to which they contribute is a meaningful way of evaluating their development.

3 Gathering pupils' views on their progress

One of the best ways to understand how pupils are progressing is simply to ask them. A major aspect of confidence, independence and resilience is what pupils think about themselves, their learning and their future. As such, asking them directly can provide a powerful complementary source of evidence to the two types of monitoring described above. More than this, though, seeking their views is itself a way of valorising pupils and prompting them to reflect on their own progress.

You can do this through your dialogue with pupils about learning day-to-day, or through holding more structured individual or whole-class discussions at various points across the year. An even more structured way to gather views would be to conduct a survey, asking pupils to express their level of agreement or disagreement with a series of simple statements. Using the same survey at several moments across the school year would offer a vivid profile of how pupils believe they're progressing in these areas, support your planning, and provide an excellent basis for conversations with them.

Use the information you gather to adjust your plan as required

Feedback should be a continuous process allowing you and your pupils to understand the current state of play and adjust course as necessary. 'Feedback', the EEF toolkit states, 'redirects or refocuses either the teacher's or the learner's actions to achieve a goal, by aligning effort and activity with an outcome'. This idea of 'aligning effort and activity with an outcome' is absolutely key: good evaluation allows you and your pupils to ensure you're targeting your effort on the areas that will make the maximum impact and making the most of every moment in the classroom. This becomes all the more powerful when pupils are actively involved in evaluating their own progress. Apart from feedback, the other top intervention that the EEF Toolkit highlights is 'meta-cognition and self-regulation': 'teaching pupils specific strategies to set goals, monitor and evaluate their own learning' (see p.106).[11]

Notes

1 Stafford-Brizard, B. (2016). *Building Blocks for Learning: A Framework for Comprehensive Student Development.* Turnaround for Children, p.4.
2 Dweck, C., Walton, G., and Cohen, G. (2011). *Academic Tenacity: Mindsets and Skills that Promote Long-Term Learning.* Seattle, WA: The Gates Foundation, p.27.
3 Education Endowment Foundation. Teaching and Learning Toolkit. Available at: educationendowmentfoundation.org.uk/resources/teaching-learning-toolkit
4 Wiliam, D. (2013). Assessment: the bridge between teaching and learning. *Voices from the Middle*, 21(2), p.15.
5 Hattie, J. (2012). *Visible Learning for Teachers: Maximizing Impact on Learning.* Abingdon: Routledge, p.182.
6 Wiliam, D. (2014). Why Teaching Will Never Be a Research-Based Profession and Why that's a Good Thing. [Lecture at ResearchED Conference]. London,

6 September 2014. Available at: www.dylanwiliam.org/Dylan_Wiliams_website/-Presentations.html
7 Hattie, J. and Yates, G. (2013). *Visible Learning and the Science of How We Learn.* Abingdon: Routledge, p.xi.
8 Farrington, C.A., Roderick, M., Allensworth, E., Nagaoka, J., Keyes, T.S., Johnson, D.W., and Beechum, N.O. (2012). *Teaching Adolescents to Become Learners. The Role of Noncognitive Factors in Shaping School Performance: A Critical Literature Review.* Chicago: University of Chicago Consortium on Chicago School Research, p.8.
9 ibid.
10 Willingham, D. (2013). Measurement of Non-Cognitive Factors. [Blog] *Daniel Willingham: Science and Education Blog.* Available at: www.danielwillingham.com/daniel-willingham-science-and-education-blog/measurement-of-non-cognitive-factors
11 See note 3 above.

6 Creating the right conditions

The purpose of this second phase is to establish a classroom culture that embodies your aims and makes pupils feel comfortable to try, take risks and make mistakes. At the heart of this culture are your relationships with pupils and the dialogue you have with them about what you're trying to achieve together.

Much of this section is simply about talking and listening to pupils: getting to know them, encouraging them, talking about their short and long term aims, and discussing the role of error and effort in learning. Although words alone aren't sufficient to shift unhelpful mindsets and build new habits, the power of classroom dialogue is often understated, especially given how little teacher time and effort it requires. The discussions you have with pupils, and the language you use, are the backdrop to everything your pupils do and can radically change the way they work. As Dweck, Walton and Cohen write: 'Even the subtlest messages educators send to students as they give them feedback, try to motivate their learning, or simply convey their own beliefs and values can shape students' motivation, making them more or less tenacious learners'.[1]

Building trusting relationships and getting to know pupils

- Be positive and friendly, whilst setting and enforcing boundaries
- Make time to get to know pupils at the start of the year
- Ask pupils for their opinion on what they enjoy and what's helped them learn in the past
- Be open about why you're doing what you're doing in lessons
- Encourage pupils to value the qualities they bring to the classroom

Providing ongoing encouragement

- Express your belief that pupils can and will achieve
- Give sincere, specific praise for effort, progress and the process of learning
- Demonstrate to pupils that you notice and value their effort
- Communicate successes to pupils' families

Sharing and refining aims with pupils

- Explicitly share your aims with the class
- Ask for their input and revise the aims together
- Agree on a common language to describe and discuss your aims

Ongoing discussion of pupils' aims and futures

- Keep aims present day-to-day
- Relate day-to-day work to longer term ambitions

Establishing a classroom culture that welcomes risk-taking and error

- Introduce pupils to the idea of a growth mindset
- Talk explicitly about mistake-making and risk-taking as crucial for learning
- Turn mistakes into opportunities for learning in the classroom

Building trusting relationships and getting to know pupils

- Be positive and friendly, whilst setting and enforcing boundaries
- Make time to get to know pupils at the start of the year
- Ask pupils for their opinion on what they enjoy and what's helped them learn in the past
- Be open about why you're doing what you're doing in lessons
- Encourage pupils to value the qualities they bring to the classroom

'If you don't trust someone you are not going to listen to them,' says Alice, 'and if you don't listen to them you're not learning from them. Some of these children have had really turbulent relationships with adults – they've been let down by people before, so that trust is so, so important.'

Her view is echoed by Daniel Willingham, who writes that the 'emotional bond between students and teacher – for better or worse – accounts for whether students learn.'[2] Similarly, in his writings on the importance of feedback, Dylan Wiliam states that 'the thing that really matters in feedback is the relationship between the student and the teacher.'[3]

This is a critical step, then, for good learning, not merely for a good atmosphere. Luke, a pupil from Dan's GCSE English class (see p.x), describes the power of strong teacher–pupil relationships:

> I think for most people in the class, he's their favourite teacher because we can just have conversations with him. Like, if it's after-school or break time you can have a conversation with him, whether it's about work or just about anything. It means that you have quite a close connection with him, and that helps my English work because it means I'm not afraid of him to judge what I am doing, because I have quite a good connection with him as a teacher but also as a person.

The value Luke attaches to just being able to have a conversation with Dan highlights the simplicity of this area. Building good relationships with pupils doesn't require irresistible charisma, an up to date knowledge of youth culture or a razor-sharp wit, it's simply about being friendly and available, asking questions and taking time to listen. Creating incidental moments to ask pupils about their lives and the things that matter to them can, from a certain perspective, seem non-essential, even a waste of learning time. However, Dweck, Walton and Cohen stress that this simple habit 'establishes an emotional safety zone' for pupils and can have a significant impact on motivation, engagement and ultimately grades. 'The perception that teachers care about their students is among the strongest predictors of student performance', they continue. There are even greater benefits for 'high-risk youth', for whom caring relationships and feeling a sense of belonging mean 'they are less likely to drop out of school or be arrested'.[4]

Be positive and friendly, whilst setting and enforcing boundaries

Pupils will respond far better to a positive, friendly manner from a teacher if it's accompanied by clear expectations of behaviour. 'It is a real cliché and I hate to use it,' says Katie, 'but I think it is really true that pupils need tough love; they need to know you care, but they also need really clear boundaries. It's about setting up a culture and being quite specific.' James makes a similar point. 'You need to set your stall out quite clearly, so say: *There are certain things I won't accept*, and never accept them. Then the kids will start to trust you because they know what they can and can't do. Relationships are built on that trust.'

It can be difficult to adopt a manner that communicates both openness and authority. Sarah told us how, when she started teaching, she 'had quite a lot of barriers up' and 'didn't quite understand the power of relationships.' Since then, without relaxing her expectations of pupils, she's become far more friendly and open, sharing details about her own life and asking pupils about theirs. When asked about the culture in Sarah's classroom today, one of her pupils told us, 'we're like a family now'. Rick, one of Lawrence's Year 8 pupils, told us that teachers should aim for a manner that's 'fun and serious at the same time.' Lawrence jokes with pupils, but he frequently adopts a sterner manner and tone of voice to challenge certain behaviours and communicate high expectations.

Nicknames

'You remember things that you enjoy and you remember people who helped you enjoy something or who made you laugh', said Chris. 'A kid would turn up to my classroom looking like a scruff and I would give them the name of a scruffy character in the book. I'd give different kids different nicknames from the books we were studying: if you call someone Tybalt, he loves that and he wants to find out what happens next to Tybalt.'

Make time to get to know pupils at the start of the year

Carve out time in the first few lessons with a new class to find out about pupils as individuals, both through conversation and through specific getting-to-know-you activities: writing you a letter, filling in a quiz or survey, drawing a map of their life, listing favourite things (see p.54 for an example). Combine this with individual conversations around school at incidental moments.

Simple and obvious as all this may sound, Dan's pupil Luke explains its value. 'He could pick any person in here and tell you a bit about them', Luke said of Dan. 'He could tell you their likes and their dislikes and who they talk to in school. It's actually important because it means a teacher doesn't just see you as their class, they see you as people that they can communicate with individually.'

John Hattie and Gregory Yates suggest being quite systematic in the way that you acquire and record this knowledge of pupils:

> Recognise the individuality of your students. Know them as real people with personal lives [...] Make written notes, a file, of what you know of their likes and values. Such knowledge is invaluable in adjusting teaching in individual feedback and remedial work.[5]

Whether or not you keep a written record or feel you can retain details without one, the key is that every single one of your pupils knows that you're interested in them and care about them.

Ask pupils for their opinion on what they enjoy and what's helped them learn in the past

While you're getting to know pupils, consult them on what they enjoy in lessons and what's helped them learn in the past. Taking the time to discuss how pupils view themselves and their learning gives you a clearer idea of how to engage them, as well as giving you a rough baseline of how confident, independent and resilient they are at the start of the year. Some of the teachers I spoke to ask pupils for feedback on lessons throughout the school year, so that they continue to have a voice in their learning.

Caveat: The aim here is to get to know pupils, hear about their past experiences and give them a voice in their learning, not to ask pupils to tell you how they learn best – a notion that strays close to the idea of pupils having different 'learning styles', a theory that has since been discredited. As the teacher, you will ultimately decide on the learning experiences that your pupils need.

Be open about why you're doing what you're doing in lessons

James S is very open with his pupils about the way he teaches and why: '*I've done this, so that you can do that.* I find that helps them – then they can see it.' He compares this to adult relationships, and the fact that people are more likely to respond positively to a request if they know the rationale behind it. 'I see us as a team,' James continues, 'and I don't know why there has to be anything secret from them in terms of what I'm expecting them to do and why I'm expecting them to do it.' James E agrees: 'I make what I'm doing quite transparent, I'm quite open, even with a Year 3 class. It hooks in so much better if you do that.'

Pupils feel respected when teachers explain the rationale behind their actions. More than that, the act of telling pupils the outcome you're trying to achieve through a given activity or routine can make that outcome more likely. Telling pupils, as Lawrence does on p.98, that you're using cold calling because you want them to become more confident expressing themselves, and want them to feel comfortable having a go even when they're unsure of the answer, will affect the way that they view and interact with that routine. The explicit narrative that accompanies your teaching can infuse activities, systems and routines with a significance and power that they wouldn't otherwise have had.

You can also, of course, ask pupils to work out the reasons why they're doing something themselves. Kayleigh regularly asks pupils: 'What is the purpose of doing this activity? Why are we doing it? Are there are other skills we're developing whilst we're doing this activity?' (see p.30). Chris extends this logic to the way that he sets and maintains expectations in the classroom more generally. 'Explaining why you're doing something gets the kids to buy in', says Chris. 'I would even say to them: *Why am I telling you off now? Why should you be silent?* If you have a reason behind it, it makes the things that they might find difficult have meaning. It's about dignity – giving them respect and dignity. The things you're asking the kids to do are for their own good, and they should know that and know why.'

Encourage pupils to value the qualities they bring to the classroom

Geoffrey Cohen has studied why certain young people don't feel they belong in an academic school environment, looking specifically at young people in minority groups 'who face negative stereotypes in school and may not feel that the attributes they value most in themselves – their sense of humor, their relationship with their family – make them valuable in the school setting.' In one study, teachers gave pupils a simple activity:

> [Students] ranked a list of personal values in terms of their importance to them. [...] They] then wrote for about 15 minutes about why their top-ranked value was important to them. [...] A few booster exercises reinforced the intervention during the year.

Compared to a control group, pupils from minority groups who participated in this activity gained better grades and were more likely to be assigned to higher sets. Cohen believes that by encouraging pupils to focus on the qualities they value most in themselves, pupils 'can "bring" these values into the school setting and thereby enhance their sense of belonging.'[6] 'Broadening their perspectives on themselves', Cohen says, 'reduces minority students' sense of threat and therefore the likeliness that they will falter'.[7] Another way to develop a sense of belonging in pupils is to connect them to older pupils who can talk frankly about feelings of not fitting in or believing you're up to par, and help them to overcome those feelings.

Case Study: Making pupils feel valued

Faced with a highly cautious and under-confident Year 10 science class, Katie made a conscious effort to get to know them, forge trusting relationships, make pupils feel valued and build their self-belief.

Palm reading

Katie asked pupils 'to trace around their hand in the very first lesson', then to write their name in the middle, and their favourite lesson, a favourite hobby and a few other personal interests and ambitions on the thumb and fingers. 'Just by doing that activity', she says, 'you could almost see them thinking: *I've got someone here who is quite interested in me as a person.*'

Seeking pupil feedback on lessons

Katie seeks feedback on her lessons, asking pupils '*What's working for you at the moment, and what isn't working for you?*' This is simple to do and gives her information on how her pupils perceive her teaching and what they think would help them learn. Furthermore, it demonstrates Katie's respect for them and invests them in the learning process. 'It boosts our confidence more,' says one pupil, 'she gets us to say what we don't like about the lesson, so she can improve on it and make the lesson more enjoyable for everyone.'

Personalised feedback cards

At a key moment in the year, Katie wrote a card to each of the members of the class, containing a short, encouraging message. 'It's information about us', says her pupil Jason. 'What we've done good, how she feels about us, and what we can do – with our picture on as well. We look at them, appreciate it and think about how we can improve.' The cards also contain a target for each of them and, when she handed them out, she asked pupils to add a note for themselves on what they want to stop, start and continue doing to improve the way they're working. This is a highly time-consuming measure, unfeasible for large numbers of pupils. However, for a particularly delicate group with low confidence, gestures like these are a way to build pupils up, to demonstrate care for them and belief in their abilities, and to help them focus on, and take greater ownership, of their goals.

Instilling belief

'I genuinely, genuinely believe they can achieve what they set their minds to,' Katie says, 'and it's just about instilling that belief for them to have a go. I will say to them: *You are in school, and you are in Year 10. All around the country there are Year 10 pupils. What's different about you? Why can't you achieve absolutely anything that anybody else can?*' Katie attempts 'to challenge the paradigms that are stuck in their heads' and are 'so entrenched that they're not conscious.'

Providing ongoing encouragement

- Express your belief that pupils can and will achieve
- Give sincere, specific praise for effort, progress and the process of learning
- Demonstrate to pupils that you notice and value their effort
- Communicate successes to pupils' families

Classroom dialogue is one of those rare beasts in education: something that takes little teacher time and effort, but can have a profound influence on the way pupils work and the aims they're focusing on. Certain kinds of praise and encouragement, in particular, can powerfully enhance pupils' motivation and sense of self-efficacy. 'Expressing positive expectations of pupils – that they can and will learn and be successful – is one of the most powerful ways to influence pupils and raise achievement', states Hay McBer's report into teacher effectiveness. 'It is one of the distinctive behaviours of high performing teachers who radiate confidence in their pupils and their potential, and never give up on them.' The act of doing this, it continues, can 'shape pupils' [. . .] perceptions of themselves'.[8]

I heard a similar message from Bushra, a pupil in the final weeks of Year 6, talking about her teacher Alice. 'Before our SAT's she would say *I know you can do it*. She's always on our side and she actually makes us think: Yes, we *can* do it . . .' I asked Bushra why hearing Alice say this made a difference. 'Sometimes words can actually affect you', she continued. 'If she thinks we can do it and she says it, it is actually going to make us want to try. We believe in what she's saying . . . You can tell from her face and the way she says it.'

Express your belief that pupils can and will achieve

'[E]ducators at every level', write Dweck, Walton and Cohen, 'can promote tenacity by sending the message, in word and deed, that their students truly belong and have great potential'.[9] As in Bushra's comment above, explicitly and frequently telling pupils that you believe that they can and will succeed can be very powerful. Lowri tries to be like a 'broken record' in her classroom, something that her pupils notice and appreciate. 'She encourages us,' says Khalil, 'so that if we don't know how to do anything she tells us *Carry on, you can get it, you can do it*. She always pushes us and then we get it because she keeps on.' Specifically expressing your belief in pupils, rather than making generically positive remarks, matters, as we heard from Paul, one of Katie's Year 10 pupils (see p.54). 'No other teacher has said: *I believe in you*', he said. 'They just say *Well done* and that's it.'

Caveat: John Hattie and Gregory Yates sound an important note of warning here. You can 'boost a child's self-efficacy through some types of verbal exhortation', they write. But simply 'telling a student *You can do it* is not an appropriate message if it conflicts with what this young person is telling him or herself.' In other words, this message needs to be delivered alongside evidence of progress, however small and incremental (see pp.77–82 for examples of teachers doing this). Bushra was only affected by Alice's encouragement because Alice had allowed her pupils to experience a feeling of academic success. Hattie and Yates recommend relating current challenges to past successes, saying for example: '*I know you can do these problems as they are just like the ones you did last week, but a bit harder.*' This 'works not so much through persuasion,' they write, 'as it does through jogging the right memories at the right time'.[10]

A study by Cohen and Garcia in the United States explored the power of expressing belief in pupils.[11] In this study, a marked piece of writing was returned to pupils with a post-it note attached. A control group received a post-it simply saying 'I'm giving you these comments so that you'll have feedback on your paper.' The other half of the pupils were given a note saying 'I'm giving you these comments because I have very high expectations and I know you can reach them.' Pupils were then told that they could revisit and improve their writing if they wanted.

Pupils who received the post-it note expressing high expectations were far more likely to revisit their essay and to improve their grade on that piece of work. The most notable finding, however, which has features in common with Cohen's values affirmation study on p.53, was that pupils in minority groups were far more affected by this intervention: 87% of white pupils who received the high expectations note chose to improve their essay compared to 62% of those who received the control note; among black pupils in the study, 72% of those who received the high expectations note reworked their essay compared to just 17% of pupils in the control group.

Paul Tough offers a wise assessment of the implications of this research:

[T]he conclusion to draw from the study is not that teachers should start slapping high-expectations Post-its on every piece of work they hand back to students. It's that teachers have a critical and potentially transformative opportunity, when dealing with students who perceive school as a threatening place, to disarm those threats by changing the way they communicate.[12]

Motivate Me

As a break halfway through long double lessons, Sarah runs a regular section called 'Motivate Me', 'a couple of minutes where we either play a motivational video or tell a motivational story.' Sarah and her pupils take turns to lead these sections and select the content. She sees these interludes as a way to encourage her pupils and 'to change the way that they think': to raise their expectations of themselves and build their self-belief.

Give sincere, specific praise for effort, progress and the process of learning

'I love that word *sombre*', we heard Andreas say to a pupil during an activity about adjectives. 'You definitely met that challenge of using some ambitious words'. To make his praise meaningful, he focuses on specific details of what his pupils have done.

Being specific and careful with the way praise is delivered can help to develop a growth mindset in pupils. We 'should praise the right things', writes Carol Dweck. 'We should praise the process (the effort, the strategies, the ideas, what went into the work), not the person.'[13] 'Praising process rather than ability sends the unspoken message that intelligence is under the student's control', writes Daniel Willingham, recommending that teachers 'make that message explicit'.[14]

Another advantage of this approach is that it enables teachers to avoid making even implicit comparisons between the achievements of different pupils. Instead, pupils compare current with past performance and feel that their progress is valued on its own terms.

Caveat: Teachers should be very wary 'of praising second-rate work', writes Daniel Willingham, as this undermines the praise and simply communicates low expectations.[15]

DIY stickers

Rebecca gives stickers to her pupils as a reward, but instead of giving out generic shop-bought stickers, she writes a short comment on a plain white label, praising a specific aspect of a pupil's effort and progress. This takes more time, but these stickers actually make it clear to pupils what they have done well and help them to see their progress. They also act as a way of communicating with pupils' families, who can see exactly what their children have done well at school and can reinforce the teacher's specific praise at home. For another example of focused praise in practice, see p.29.

Demonstrate to pupils that you notice and value their effort

When you're trying to encourage all pupils to take risks and participate in your classroom, you need simple ways of showing them that you're noticing their efforts. This could be as simple as a smile, a nod, a thumbs up, a quick comment, or a star on a star chart. During stretching discussions with his least confident classes, Lawrence writes pupils' names on the whiteboard as an easy way of showing them that he's noticing and valuing their participation. He doesn't make a fuss about this and keeps his attention on the discussion – he simply makes a note of their names and ticks them as pupils make further contributions. This is easy to do, acknowledges pupils' willingness to take a risk, and encourages further participation.

For her part, Elizabeth has a 'no hands up' rule in some discussions and calls on pupils instead. When you're trying to build pupil confidence 'it's not helpful to have hands waving in the air', she says. Many pupils in her class have limited English and 'there's nothing worse,' she continues, 'than being that kid who's sitting there trying their hardest to think of a sentence – when they already don't know the words in English – and having somebody's arm waving in front of their face.' If other pupils are vying for the teacher's attention and parading their own confidence, there's a risk that certain children want 'to dig a hole into the ground and crawl into it whenever somebody asks them a question'.

Communicate successes to pupils' families

Most teachers strongly agree that informing pupils' families about their children's progress and successes is a powerful way of motivating pupils and showing them that you care about them. Most teachers also agree that this is time-consuming and hard to do regularly and systematically.

Lawrence was shocked into action in this area after he gave one of his classes a survey, asking how they felt about him, his classroom and their learning. He reviewed the results and was surprised to realise that his pupils didn't think he cared about them and their lives as much as he felt he did. 'I took it as read that they understood that I was invested in them as human beings and invested in their life,' he said, 'and actually that's not always the case.' He was further struck by the fact that, prior to the survey, he hadn't been able to discern the mismatch between his own and his pupils' perceptions.

To make it clearer that he cared about his pupils, Lawrence decided to dedicate more effort to communicating their successes to their families. 'I can tell them they're brilliant in class a million times, but it means so much more to them if their parents hear it too', he told us. 'So, I started to do that more. I call home, I send postcards home, I send letters home. I'm in regular contact with their parents now.' Labour-intensive as this undoubtedly is, it binds families into their children's learning and is a form of recognition that many pupils find exceedingly meaningful and motivating.

Sharing and refining aims with pupils

- **Explicitly share your aims with the class**
- **Ask for their input and revise the aims together**
- **Agree on a common language to describe and discuss your aims**

'One of the most transformational things I ever did was just say: *This is my target for the class*', Dan told me. 'That changed everything and gave a sense of purpose to everything they do.' The act of sharing ambitious academic targets with a class can embolden pupils and help to build their confidence. The moment acquires even greater power if your conversations extend beyond the academic – to the other mindsets and skills that pupils need, and to discussions about their broader aims for the future. If you then consult pupils, and refine and finalise these aims together, it's more likely that they will feel ownership of these goals, and, ultimately, direct and monitor their own progress towards them. Missing this step out, and keeping your aims to yourself (or only sharing their expected grade), can result in pupils having a narrow perspective of what they're striving for in the classroom, and approaching learning with less energy and ambition as a consequence.

Explicitly share your aims with the class

The first step here is simply to tell your class about the bold aims you have for them. 'Quite often when I first meet a class,' says Lucy, 'a grade C is what they're aiming for and you have to work with them to make them want to aim higher.' 'Sometimes', she continues, 'it's about saying to someone, *No, no – there's something else you can do, there's something higher you can achieve*, and making them really push themselves. So I'll show them what I want them to get. I'll say, *This is my vision for you, this is what I think you should get next year* and then just be constantly pushing them towards that.'

Ambitious academic goals can catalyse motivation and engagement, but they can also appear daunting. Discussing them in conjunction with a conversation about developing the skills, mindsets and habits that underpin academic progress can make them seem more manageable and put them in the context of a broader effort. To cohere the spectrum of aims that she has for her pupils, Becky frames these conversations in terms of 'being a good mathematician'. 'By this I don't mean *getting the right answer*,' she told me, 'but thinking logically, recognising errors, not giving up, communicating clearly [...] I am quite explicit about what I value in mathematicians, so that pupils know what habits I expect them to aspire to.'

Ask for their input and revise the aims together

Firming up your aims for pupils is best done in conversation with them. Once you've shared your own vision for them, ask them about their hopes, short and long term. Through that conversation, and perhaps through written brainstorms, you can agree on both the academic progress you're aiming for and the growth in confidence, independence and resilience. Doing this means that pupils are not only aware of what they're aiming for, but genuinely invested in those goals.

Failing to set ambitious targets with pupils can seriously limit what they strive for in the classroom and why they even think they're there. If, instead of being focused on one task after another, students are consciously working towards the future they want, they will approach their studies differently.

Agree on a common language to describe and discuss your aims

There's merit in attaching specific terms to the mindsets, skills and habits that you're working on with pupils so that everyone uses the same words to talk about the same things. This may sound unnecessary but, without a common language, communication can quickly become muddled and imprecise. The language on the outcomes flowchart (p.6) is a good starting point, although you might decide on different labels with your pupils, as in the examples below.

Class values

Ally told us that she wanted her pupils 'to believe that they can be a success and believe that they can do whatever they want to do'. She was concerned that they lacked self-confidence and felt that part of the problem was that she didn't have the 'language to talk to the children about it'. To combat this she developed and introduced five values – the five Rs – into her classroom:

- Resilience
- Respect
- Responsibility
- Being Remarkable
- Making the Right choices

To introduce them:

- She launched them with her pupils, discussing what each of the values means and coming up with definitions together
- She created a large permanent display on the classroom wall, showing each of the values alongside its definition
- And she used those five terms as the basis for conversations with pupils about their work and their overall approach to school: 'Are you making the right choice?' for example, or 'Are you being resilient? What is resilient? It means never giving up, even if things are hard.'

Many classes have overarching rules or values, but the distinctive point here is the way that Ally uses these terms to provide 'a universal language' for the personal qualities her pupils need to be successful. Her class values are 'something that they can cling to, because we use these words all of the time.'

Learnosaurs

Nicole wanted to give her reception pupils a structure and language for reflecting on their learning. She saw another teacher give a presentation on 'Learnosaurs', a series of dinosaurs named after different skills, and borrowed the idea, personalising the dinosaurs for the skills she wanted to see in her classroom. She introduced them to her pupils and displayed the dinosaurs and their descriptions on the classroom wall:

- Try-a-tops: *I try my best and never give up*
- Share-a-dactyl: *I share my ideas and resources*
- Explore-a-saur: *I explore everything around me*
- Ask-a-raptor: *I ask questions and find things out*
- Think-o-docus: *I think carefully about what I learn*
- Solve-o-saurus Rex: *I work hard to solve problems*
- Stick-a-saurus: *I stick at tasks and persevere*

'The dinosaurs were introduced one at a time', says Nicole. 'We'd meet it and find out how to be that dinosaur.' The adults in the room then made a point of noticing when children were showing a particular dinosaur skill and would ask them, in whole-class discussions, to talk about what they had done.

Once the children understood the dinosaurs and had got used to talking about them, Nicole began to ask children to plan out their Choosing Time, selecting a dinosaur skill they wanted to work on. The children would decide on a skill, go away to 'do some of their own learning' and then 'come back to the carpet and review what they'd done', referring to the dinosaurs to reflect on the skills that they and others had shown.

'Initially during review a child would say *I built a sandcastle*', says Nicole. 'After the introduction of the dinosaurs we would have a reflective narrative: *I worked in the sandpit, I wanted to build a sandcastle but the sand was too dry so I was a Solve-o-saurus Rex and we got some water. We needed a lot of water but we were Stick-a-saurus and kept going until the sand felt right. The bucket was really heavy so we asked for help by being Ask-a-raptors. I had to share the bucket with a friend as there were so many people in the sandpit so I was a Share-a-dactyl too.*' Later on in the year, she and her teaching assistants assigned children 'a challenge dinosaur – a behaviour that we wanted to encourage or didn't see a lot of'.

Ultimately, Nicole explains, the dinosaurs' 'key role is to be a reflective tool with which pupils can independently consider their learning and progress', she says; to help them 'explicitly talk about the characteristics of effective learning' and 'reflect on what they have done, what they have learnt, and how they learnt it'.

Ongoing discussion of pupils' aims and futures

- **Keep aims present day-to-day**
- **Relate day-to-day work to longer term ambitions**

Your aims should filter down into everything that happens in the classroom. Discussing them regularly can help pupils to connect the present moment to the bigger picture, and build intrinsic motivation to succeed in school and beyond. It's not enough to discuss what you're trying to achieve once at the start of the year. To make an impact, this conversation needs to be a constant feature of classroom life. This requires very little time and effort and can be peppered into teaching at incidental moments.

Keep aims present day-to-day

More than anything, keeping your aims present in the classroom means talking about them: frequently relating the day-to-day details of the classroom to the goals you've agreed with pupils. This dialogue can be reinforced by displays or other physical prompts.

Dan keeps his aims present by regularly returning to the questions '*Why are you here? Why are we doing this?*' with his pupils. 'I always taught my kids that the most important question in the world is *Why?*' he told me.

> **Caveat:** Ambitious longer term aims can focus the mind and increase pupil motivation. However, they need to be twinned with challenging but achievable shorter term goals so that pupils can see a path from where they are now to where they're trying to go. These shorter term goals are themselves exceedingly motivating. 'We will exert strong efforts to perform at a high level, calling upon hidden and guarded reserves of effort, once we become confident that worthwhile goals are achievable in the short term', write Hattie and Yates.[16]

Relate day-to-day work to longer term ambitions

Pupils may be very ambitious, but they may not have a clear idea of the steps they need to take to realise those ambitions, or of how their day-to-day work in the classroom relates to them. At the start of the year Katie asks her pupils 'to think about a vision statement for themselves', asking them not only 'What are you going to achieve this year?', but also 'What are you going to achieve in your life?'

Envisaging long term hopes and how you'll get there can be motivating and provide clarity on how to approach decisions and situations in the short term. Katie pushes her pupils to consider how the effort they make day-to-day relates to long term success. As they embark on a set of practice questions, she tells them that 'working hard on those questions adds up to great results, those results add up to you doing what you want to do – you know that.' Dweck, Walton and Cohen write that long term goals 'even when they are still developing, can provide a reason for students to adopt and commit to learning goals in school. This is because students who are working with purpose feel that they are learning so that they can become the kind of person they would like to be and contribute something of value to the world.'[17]

Lowri maintains an explicit, ongoing dialogue with her pupils about the future. 'Just talking about their future all the time means they are actually thinking about it', she says, 'and I'm not sure how much they were before. I mean, they are only 8 and 9 so it's still pipe dreams, but they're important to have.' The point of this is to equip pupils to make good decisions, and to connect the effort that pupils are making day-to-day with the longer term – a connection that can be difficult to feel, even as pupils move through secondary school. 'Yes we have a learning journey and it lasts from Monday to Friday,' says Lowri, 'but it's all about a bigger journey for them. It's about having all the tools they can now to make the choices that they want to make when they are older.'

Caveats:

- There's a risk of sucking the pleasure out of learning by over-emphasising the utility of good results for future success. There's a balance to be struck.
- Unless young people feel secure and successful in the classroom, these kinds of discussions can feel tokenistic or unreal. They need to be founded on strong relationships and good learning.
- Dweck, Walton and Cohen caution that long term goals may not be motivating in the classroom if pupils are envisaging a future in which their level of academic achievement is not relevant, 'such as acting, athletics, or music.'[18] That's not to say that pupils shouldn't have these goals, rather that teachers should be aware that they could lead to pupils discounting the value of academic effort and achievement. You may need to approach these pupils to discuss and confirm the relevance and value of classroom work for them and their aspirations.

Establishing a classroom culture that welcomes risk-taking and error

- **Introduce pupils to the idea of a growth mindset**
- **Talk explicitly about mistake-making and risk-taking as crucial for learning**
- **Turn mistakes into opportunities for learning in the classroom**

'If you don't have confidence and you don't have resilience,' Elizabeth says, 'how on earth are you meant to take the risk to put pen to paper? How on earth are you meant to put your neck on the line and look like a banana in front of everybody else by getting something wrong?' These questions animate the way that Elizabeth teaches. She sees building these characteristics as the essential 'groundwork' for good learning in other areas. 'If you don't take risks, then you will never learn anything', she says.

It's of paramount importance that pupils feel comfortable enough to take risks, attempt difficult work and make mistakes. If they're not being challenged, they're not learning. Daniel Willingham describes the key messages for pupils as follows:

> If you want to increase your intelligence, you have to challenge yourself. That means taking on tasks that are a bit beyond your reach, and that means you may very well fail, at least the first time around. [...] Failure means you're about to learn something. You're going to find out that there's something you didn't understand or didn't know how to do.[19]

Introduce pupils to the idea of a growth mindset

Growth mindset, a concept put forward by Carol Dweck, relates to whether students believe their intelligence is a 'fixed trait' or 'something they could develop';[20] whether, in other words, they're motivated by a desire to take risks and learn, or a desire to avoid risks and appear successful. Dylan Wiliam describes the growth mindset's importance in relation to students' willingness to interact positively with feedback:

> Students must understand that they are *not* born with talent (or lack of it) and that their personalities do *not* determine whether or not they are "good at math" or "good at writing." Rather, ability is incremental. The harder you work, the smarter you get. Once students begin to understand this "growth mindset" as Carol Dweck calls it, students are much more likely to embrace feedback from their teachers.[21]

A first step in supporting pupils to develop a growth mindset is simply talking about it explicitly in the classroom and supporting pupils to understand the relationship between effort and attainment. This was something I saw in Joe's history classroom. 'I want to build a growth mindset', he told me. 'There's this idea that *I'm thick, I can't do it, I'm not good enough*. So I try to build in all of my kids that working hard is the key: trying and putting effort into things, looking where you're at and working out how to get better. I want them to carry that through their whole life.' Joe explicitly talks to pupils about the importance of a growth mindset and challenges pupils with fixed ideas about themselves. 'It's like *You're not naughty, you're not thick. That is not the truth. No one is thick and no one is naughty. If you want to get better behaved, practise at it. If you want to get better at your work, practise at it.*'

As well as communicating these kinds of messages to pupils, Dweck, Walton and Cohen recommend the following methods for helping pupils to absorb the idea of a growth mindset:

- Explain to pupils how the brain works: how it makes new connections and gets more intelligent when working on challenging tasks
- Ask older pupils to talk to your pupils about the connection between intelligence and hard work
- Ask pupils to communicate the idea of a growth mindset to younger pupils themselves, in person or in writing[22]

For an example of a teacher helping pupils to visualise and overcome a fixed mindset see p.83.

Caveat: Dweck is careful to point out that we don't simply have a fixed mindset or a growth mindset: building a growth mindset is a gradual, ongoing process and might be something we have in certain areas of our life and not in others. In an article debunking myths about the growth mindset, she wrote:

Let's legitimize the fixed mindset. Let's acknowledge that (1) we're all a mixture of fixed and growth mindsets, (2) we will probably always be, and (3) if we want to move closer to a growth mindset in our thoughts and practices, we need to stay in touch with our fixed-mindset thoughts and deeds.[23]

This is an important point for teachers to bear in mind. It's easier for someone to declare that they have a growth mindset, or to explain what the term means, than to consistently think and act in a way that's informed by one. Likewise pupils may have a growth mindset about certain aspects of their learning and not others. A growth mindset isn't simply something pupils either have or don't have.

Mindset Diamond 9

Becky told me how she gave each of her Year 10 classes a 'Diamond 9' (nine slips of paper to be arranged into a diamond shape with the most important item at the top and the least important at the bottom) and asked pupils to order nine different factors in terms of the impact they would have on their GSCE grade. 'Most of my pupils in Set 1 put things like "growth mindset" or "regular work" at the top,' she said, 'but the lower down the setting system a pupil was, the more likely they were to put "natural ability". As they didn't feel they had that natural ability, they didn't think they could do much about their GCSE grade. After that, we tried to be even more explicit about attitudes and behaviours that would help them to build a growth mindset.'

Talk explicitly about mistake-making and risk-taking as crucial for learning

Intertwined with pupils' fixed or growth mindsets are their attitudes to finding work difficult and making mistakes. Without a growth mindset, pupils are likely to see struggling with work as a sign of failure; even if they're convinced by the idea of the growth mindset, if they don't believe that struggle and mistake-making are an important part of learning, they may give up when work becomes difficult and fall back into old habits. Pupils need to know, in Angela Duckworth's words, that 'the emotions of confusion and frustration are typical, and possibly essential, to learning'.[24] This awareness, combined with a growth mindset, should, Carol Dweck says, lead to children saying: '*Wow, this is when I'm getting smarter*' when they attempt challenging work.[25]

As before, the first step here is simply to talk openly with pupils about the experience of making mistakes, the discomfort that can accompany it, and the value that error has for learning. One of Patrick's pupils told me about the way that he talks about mistakes: 'He said when he was young, he used to make mistakes all the time, but he learnt from his mistakes and he got better at working with his mistakes.' Patrick turned this subject into a major focus for his class, and established a frank, daily dialogue about the importance of mistake making. Now his pupils talk positively about the subject. 'Next time I'll get the right answer – because I know I made a mistake but I learnt from it as well,' said one. 'Sometimes mistakes can be bad,' said another, 'but not when you are making a maths mistake or something, because you learn from it and that's what

I do. I don't get really frustrated or anything.' In a similar vein, Becky told me that she is deliberately 'a bit OTT in praising mistakes' in order 'to normalise them, and to turn them into positive experiences'. All of this chimes with the words of the philosopher Daniel Dennett: 'The chief trick to making good mistakes is not to hide them – especially not from yourself.'[26]

Turn mistakes into opportunities for learning in the classroom

'I'm a massive fan of children valuing their own and other peoples' mistakes,' says Becky, 'and using these as learning experiences.' For Becky, this also extends to being comfortable with the fact that sometimes we forget things and need to go back to topics we thought we'd already mastered. 'Children – and adults – forget a lot', she says, 'so I think it's important to be okay with forgetting things, as long as you then turn that into a learning moment.'

When pupils recognise that mistakes are an essential part of good learning, and not a regrettable lapse, they are more likely to embrace challenging learning experiences and more likely to share their struggles as learning opportunities for others. The important step here is to take time in your classroom to review mistakes with pupils, talk about that experience, and then highlight the learning. This can be done as mistakes occur, or in a regular slot, such as the 'Best Mistake of the Day' routine in Lian's classroom (p.24). Another, complementary, approach is to model making mistakes for pupils and then talk through how to turn that experience into a positive, productive opportunity to learn. See p.68 for a case study on celebrating and learning from mistakes.

Popcorn

Mistakes 'are often the best moments for whole-class learning', says Becky, 'and eventually pupils tend to volunteer them rather than you having to find examples.' After tests, Becky goes through the papers with pupils and invites them to 'popcorn out of their seats to share any silly mistakes and warn classmates against doing similar things wrong in future.'

Classic Mistakes

'We've got a sort of policy,' says Grace, one of Becky's pupils, 'that if we're doing work and Miss spots that someone has done an error a lot of people would have made, she would share it with the whole-class so no one does it again. It's a fun way of doing it so that you'll remember it.' Becky calls these 'Classic Mistakes' and accentuates their value for learning when she shares them. Using this system, making mistakes is 'not much of an embarrassment,' says her pupil Jane. 'It's just another way that we can learn.'

Case Study: We lvoe mistakes

'When I first came to this school, behaviour was a major problem,' says Jessica. She thought it was due to her pupils 'not being willing to give things a go and not having high expectations of themselves.' Her aim was for pupils to be 'learners that want to try and have a go at things, to take chances, to be resilient when things don't go right – and be able to learn from that and move on and move upwards.' To make her pupils more comfortable with the idea of having a go and making mistakes she took the following steps.

Establishing a class motto

Jessica has her class motto, 'We Lvoe Mistakes', pasted in large letters above her whiteboard. 'I wanted to have *We Love Mistakes* as our class ethos,' she says, 'because it builds that confidence, that resilience to persevere, to persist through challenges.' Having this message so prominently displayed – written with its own mischievous spelling error – foregrounds its importance and immediately sets the tone for her classroom.

Broadening this principle beyond academic work

Jessica stresses that her motto 'encompasses everything that they do in school', and can apply equally to poor behaviour. She tells pupils that behaviour is also 'something that they can change' and is within their control.

Having a constant dialogue with pupils about the value and importance of mistake making

The class motto isn't just a sign above the whiteboard. The theme of mistakes – how we feel when we make a mistake, and how we learn from mistakes – is a constant refrain in her classroom. She embeds the motto by returning to this subject daily with pupils, sometimes for a proper discussion, sometimes in fleeting moments when someone is struggling or makes a mistake.

Being comfortable making mistakes, and talking about your own mistakes, in front of pupils

Jessica discusses her own experiences of making mistakes with her class, modelling a healthy attitude, but also admitting how uncomfortable she sometimes feels too. We may 'feel uncomfortable', she tells them, 'but part of being a lifelong learner and being able to learn and grow as people is that we need to be able to celebrate these things.'

Sharing and learning from specific mistakes

'Anytime you make a mistake, Miss always helps us to fix it by showing the class your book', says one of her pupils. As well as having an ongoing conversation with her pupils about mistakes, Jessica also actively encourages pupils to share mistakes they've made so that she can discuss specific examples. The class takes time regularly, she says, to 'look at some mistakes on the white board and see what the children have done, where they've gone wrong, how this is a good mistake and how we can learn from it.' 'It's so we don't get angry about it', another pupil said, 'and then make a fuss over it and regret what we did'.

Notes

1 Dweck, C., Walton, G., and Cohen, G. (2011). *Academic Tenacity: Mindsets and Skills that Promote Long-Term Learning.* Seattle, WA: The Gates Foundation, p.29.
2 Willingham, D. (2009). *Why Don't Students Like School?* San Francisco: Jossey-Bass, p.65.
3 Wiliam, D. (2014). Is the Feedback You're Giving Students Helping or Hindering? [Blog] *Dylan Wiliam Center Blog.* Available at: www.dylanwiliamcenter.com/is-the-feedback-you-are-giving-students-helping-or-hindering
4 Dweck, C., Walton, G., and Cohen, G. (2011). *Academic Tenacity: Mindsets and Skills that Promote Long-Term Learning.* Seattle, WA: The Gates Foundation, p.31.
5 Hattie, J., and Yates, G. (2013). *Visible Learning and the Science of How We Learn.* Abingdon: Routledge, p.225.
6 Dweck, C., Walton, G., and Cohen, G. (2011). *Academic Tenacity: Mindsets and Skills that Promote Long-Term Learning.* Seattle, WA: The Gates Foundation, pp.18–19.
7 Cohen, G. (2012). Cited in The Value of "Values Affirmation". [Blog] *Insights by Stanford Business.* Available at: www.gsb.stanford.edu/insights/value-values-affirmation
8 Hay McBer. (2000). Research into Teacher Effectiveness: A Model of Teacher Effectiveness. Department for Education and Employment, p.36.

9 Dweck, C., Walton, G., and Cohen, G. (2011). *Academic Tenacity: Mindsets and Skills that Promote Long-Term Learning*. Seattle, WA: The Gates Foundation, p.32.

10 Hattie, J., and Yates, G. (2013). *Visible Learning and the Science of How We Learn*. Abingdon: Routledge, p.221.

11 Yeager, D., Purdie-Vaughns, V., Garcia, J., Apfel, N., Brzustoski, P., Master, A., Hessert, W., Williams, M., and Cohen, G. (2014). Breaking the cycle of mistrust: wise interventions to provide critical feedback across the racial divide. *Journal of Experimental Psychology: General*, 143(2).

12 Tough, P. (2016). *Helping Children Succeed: What Works and Why*. 1st ed. [PDF], p.100.

13 Dweck, C. (2004). Cited in How Can Teachers Develop Students' Motivation – and Success? [Online interview] *Education World*. Available at: www.educationworld.com/a_issues/chat/chat010.shtml

14 Willingham, D. (2009). *Why Don't Students Like School?* San Francisco: Jossey-Bass, p.183.

15 ibid. p.186.

16 Hattie, J., and Yates, G. (2013). *Visible Learning and the Science of How We Learn*. Abingdon: Routledge, p.xiv.

17 Dweck, C., Walton, G., and Cohen, G. (2011). *Academic Tenacity: Mindsets and Skills that Promote Long-Term Learning*. Seattle, WA: The Gates Foundation, p.10.

18 ibid.

19 Willingham, D. (2009). *Why Don't Students Like School?* San Francisco: Jossey-Bass, p.184.

20 Dweck, C. (2006). *Mindset: The New Psychology of Success*. New York: Ballantine Books, p.57.

21 Wiliam, D. (2014). Is the Feedback You're Giving Students Helping or Hindering? [Blog] *Dylan Wiliam Center Blog*. Available at: www.dylanwiliamcenter.com/is-the-feedback-you-are-giving-students-helping-or-hindering

22 Dweck, C., Walton, G., and Cohen, G. (2011). *Academic Tenacity: Mindsets and Skills that Promote Long-Term Learning*. Seattle, WA: The Gates Foundation, pp.14–18.

23 Dweck, C. (2015). Carol Dweck Revisits the 'Growth Mindset'. [Online] *Education Week*. Available at: www.edweek.org/ew/articles/2015/09/23/carol-dweck-revisits-the-growth-mindset.html

24 Duckworth, A. (2015). Research Statement. [Online] *The Duckworth Lab*. Accessed May 2015. Available at: https://sites.sas.upenn.edu/duckworth/pages/research-statement

25 Dweck, C. (2013). Growth Mindset – Interview with Dr. Carol Dweck & Dr. Greg Walton. [Online] *Coursera: Teaching Character and Creating Positive Classrooms*. Available at: www.coursera.org/learn/teaching-character/lecture/zh6vE/growth-mindset-interview-with-dr-carol-dweck-dr-greg-walton

26 Dennett, D. (2013). *Intuition Pumps and Other Tools for Thinking*. New York: W. W. Norton & Company, p.22.

7 Building new habits

This phase is about how to build on your classroom culture and ensure that your aims filter down into the minutiae of classroom activity. With thought and planning, even the smallest systems and routines can be used to give pupils regular practice of key skills and enable them to build the habits and mindsets that will make them confident, independent, resilient learners.

To develop these new ways of thinking and behaving – through a process of 'intentional habituation', as Lesley Brown put it on p.21 – pupils need a blend of intense support and intense challenge. They need to feel encouraged and they need you to demand their best; they need new tools and strategies, then they need to be challenged to use them to solve their own problems; they need to know you're on hand, then they need to be handed ever greater responsibility for their learning. The support teachers need to offer is, in the words of Dweck, Walton and Cohen, 'subtle but sufficient – just enough so that the student can advance, seemingly on his or her own', and it's comprised of 'two forms of scaffolding: the scaffolding of students' cognitive learning and the scaffolding of their motivation to learn.'[1]

The right proportions of support and challenge, of being held afloat and thrown into the deep end, can catalyse a virtuous cycle: self-help strategies and safety nets give pupils the confidence to tackle challenging work; in turn, being successful at challenging work further builds their confidence and appetite for challenge. Ultimately, the aim is that new habits take root and pupils develop deep confidence, independence and resilience, which endure beyond the influence of a particular teacher or context. Until that occurs, support in the classroom allows them to act *as though they have* the skills and mindsets they need, and to practise and strengthen them in academically challenging situations. William James, writing about the process of embedding new habits in his *Talks to teachers on psychology*, says that pupils need to 'have a series of uninterrupted successes [in applying a particular habit], until repetition has fortified it to such a degree as to enable it to cope [...] under any circumstances'.[2]

Supporting pupils

Enabling pupils to experience success and celebrating their progress

- Challenge pupils and enable them to experience success
- Use feedback to show pupils the progress they're making
- Enable pupils to keep track of their progress
- Celebrate pupil progress

Teaching pupils strategies to overcome challenges

- Give pupils a simple framework to follow when they're stuck
- Teach pupils to select and use resources independently
- Support pupils to manage impulses and deal with pressure

Enabling pupils to support, and seek support from, one another

- Create an atmosphere of mutual support and responsibility
- Teach pupils to give one another feedback

Challenging pupils

Demanding maximum effort and quality from pupils

- Inject pace and urgency into lessons
- Have exacting standards of behaviour and personal organisation
- Expect pupils' best effort and participation
- Create an academic atmosphere in the classroom

Providing pupils with opportunities to work independently

- Give pupils structured periods of independence
- Make homework as meaningful as possible
- Teach pupils to practise effectively

Expecting pupils to monitor and direct their own progress

- Give pupils an active role in monitoring their progress
- Allow pupils to select and adjust the level of challenge
- Teach pupils to plan out work and set goals for themselves

Enabling pupils to experience success and celebrating their progress

- **Challenge pupils and enable them to experience success**
- **Use feedback to show pupils the progress they're making**
- **Enable pupils to keep track of their progress**
- **Celebrate pupil progress**

'I tell them they are going to learn something,' says James S, 'and then I make them prove it to both me and themselves. Then, at the end, you get that trust.' Nicky says something very similar: 'If somebody tells you that you are doing well at something, and they show you evidence, it is going to give you more of an incentive to carry on and to get even better.' I heard the same thing from Mark: 'When they know they can be successful, it's worth taking a gamble and trying. It's not worth the risk of trying something if you know there's a high chance of failure. So the big thing was showing them that they could be successful, and then starting to boost their confidence.'

The surest way to build self-efficacy and inspire greater effort is to enable pupils to experience success, notice the progress they are making, and then to celebrate this progress with them. John Hattie and Gregory Yates write that self-efficacy increases when pupils 'gain the evidence that their efficacy beliefs about themselves were correct'. The idea of pupils having 'evidence' is key. The more tangibly pupils can see the progress they're making, and the more sincerely that progress is celebrated, the more their appetite for further challenges will increase. 'When students can say, with evidence, "I am a learner",' Hattie and Yates continue, 'it is more likely they will invest in learning, and get pleasure from learning.'[3]

This is the engine room of the whole process of developing confidence, independence and resilience: pupils taking a risk, experiencing success, and then choosing to invest further effort to attempt further challenges.

Challenge pupils and enable them to experience success

Pupils need work that is achievable, but at the edge of what they're capable of; they should struggle, but be able to succeed with effort. Pitching work at the right level, and providing the right balance of support and autonomy, can be a delicate process, especially if pupils have a tendency to give up and have few resources to support themselves. 'In classes where the majority of pupils have lower prior attainment,' says Becky, 'I'm probably more cautious and might set the lesson up in a way that is more likely to guarantee success. I'm more wary about them having a bad lesson and closing down over certain topics.' That said,

Becky is also conscious of 'how damaging it can be to not challenge pupils enough, both in terms of the questions they're given and in terms of the learning behaviours you expect from them.' It's crucial to challenge pupils, but in a structured way that enables them to overcome it and succeed. 'I try not to protect pupils from challenge', Becky says. 'It's about exposure – building them up to be able to handle harder and harder problems.' You can find techniques for supporting pupils to overcome challenges in the next section, on p.83.

You're aiming for a situation in which pupils 'feel like they are doing something well and that their effort is giving them rewards,' says Mark, 'and that, when they walk into that room and try, something good will come of it.' And then, when pupils start to experience success, 'they start wanting more of it', Lucy told me. 'And when some people do that, they start bringing everyone else along with them. It's a snowball effect.' Ron Berger describes the effect on a pupil of completing a truly high quality piece of work as 'transformational'. 'Once a student sees that he or she is capable of excellence,' he writes, 'that student is never quite the same. There is a new self-image, a new notion of possibility. There is an appetite for excellence. After students have had a taste of excellence, they're never quite satisfied with less.'[4]

Success first thing

For the newest arrivals to her class, and for those lacking confidence, Elizabeth arranges simple, achievable tasks first thing every morning, often focused on building vocabulary. This gives shakier pupils a 'comfortable and accessible start to the day'. 'They should all experience success,' she says, 'and that needs to start right at the start of the day.' The experience of making an effort, being successful and feeling more confident makes pupils more willing to attempt more taxing material throughout the day.

Use feedback to show pupils the progress they're making

'The children think they can't,' says Sam of her pupils. Her approach to changing this mentality is to 'show them the progress they are making' so that 'they know that they can be successful.' 'It doesn't matter what level they are at,' she adds, 'they can still be successful and I want them to know that.'

Feedback is perhaps a teacher's most powerful tool for developing their pupils' confidence and willingness to invest effort in their work. Sam deliberately and constantly highlights and celebrates small successes in her marking and verbal feedback, with individuals and in front of the whole class. 'Even if they're small steps,' she says, 'show them the progress that they have made. Even if it's *You were a P6, but now you're a P7* or *Now you've put a finger space*. Little tiny steps: *You've worked really hard on that, now you can do it.*' At a basic level, what Sam is describing is simply the process of giving pupils feedback on their progress. But what distinguishes her approach, is her resolve to use assessment as the moment when she deliberately and explicitly tries to build pupil confidence and encourage further effort. Sam's approach chimes with advice from the American Psychological Association's recent paper, 'Top 20 Principles from Psychology for Teaching and Learning':

> When students are learning a new task or struggling with an existing one, frequent praise following small degrees of improvement is very important, and when progress is evident, encouragement to persist can matter a great deal. Targeted feedback can also motivate students to continue to practice learning a new skill.[5]

Dweck, Walton and Cohen remark that 'substantive feedback' as opposed to just 'a grade, checkmark, or simple evaluation ("good work"), benefits students' performance and task motivation.' A conversation or a handwritten comment suggesting how to improve provide evidence 'of the teacher's commitment to learning and belief in the student's capacity for growth.'[6]

Enable pupils to keep track of their progress

As well as providing feedback to pupils, it can be powerful to provide them with ways to monitor their own progress over the course of a challenging task and notice the small steps on the way to success. This can be as simple as providing pupils with clear, specific success criteria (see p.23). Success criteria allow students to see 'the gap between where they are and where they need to be',[7] write Hattie and Yates, and 'can assist in recalibrating [their] current conceptions of proficiency'.[8] They show pupils the route through the larger task they're engaged in, giving them a sense of achievement, and boosting their self-efficacy, en route.

'I make the assessment quite transparent', says James E, 'I make it very obvious how to do well.' James always displays very simple, specific success criteria, which enable his pupils to focus their efforts on the things that count in each lesson and act 'like a tick list for them'. As pupils meet each of the criteria, they have a palpable sense of their progress. Little by little, these small successes reinforce their belief that they can achieve. Every Friday, James reviews the full week's learning with his class, going over the success criteria they've met to make pupils aware of the progress they're making. 'They love it, it's like collecting tokens', he says, 'but I try and bring it back to *What does that actually mean?*'

Phrasing learning objectives as questions

Hayley phrases her learning objectives as big questions. At the start of her science lessons, her pupils write them out, leaving three lines blank between each one. 'As we go through the lesson,' she says, 'each task will be tailored specifically to each learning objective. Then, as we finish the task, they answer it like an exam question.' As they are answering the question, she displays levelled criteria so that pupils can see precisely what's expected at their target grade, and try to push themselves beyond it.

Pausing to answer a question after each chunk of the lesson not only consolidates pupils' learning and creates a resource to which they can return, it also makes their progress tangible and gives pupils regular opportunities to stop and take stock of their achievements. 'It's not rocket science,' Hayley says, 'and I'm sure a lot of people do it, but it means that each task that I do is really obviously channelled and the kids know where they are in the lesson the whole way through; it's a constant narrative of the lesson that's really easy to follow for both me and them.'

Progress charts

At the start of lessons, Lucy displays her success criteria as a progress chart: a list of the key steps that pupils will take throughout the lesson. She gives pupils a copy of this list so that they can tick items off as they achieve them. When I visited her, this was the chart she'd given her pupils:

State the upper and lower bounds of values rounded to 1 decimal place/3 significant figures	Grade C
Use this to calculate upper and lower bounds of perimeters	Grade B
Apply this to find upper and lower bounds of areas and in context	Grade A
Complete complex questions and round to a suitable degree of accuracy	Grade A*

'You're all going to get your progress chart of the different things I want you to look at today – it's going up in level of skill', she explained at the start of the lesson. 'This is what we're looking to do today – tick it off as you've done it, just as we normally do.' Lucy's progress charts make success criteria an active force in the lesson and build pupil self-efficacy by giving them a way of seeing and recording their progress.

Celebrate pupil progress

As well as showing pupils evidence of their achievements, it's also highly motivating to pause and celebrate the progress they're making, whether through in-class presentations, awards, praise (see p.56), communication with families (see p.59), displays (see p.25 and p.32) or other routines.

Ron Berger believes that the process of pupils sharing and presenting their best work is both a way of celebrating progress and a confidence-building challenge in its own right. You can't tell children 'to be more confident or self-assured or have more intellectual courage,' he says. 'The way kids learn that is by continually being compelled and supported to take risks – by sharing their work with their parents, by sharing their work with groups, by speaking out in class, by presenting their work. When they first have to engage like that, they are nervous, they need support, they cry – but eventually they develop the confidence and they do it.'[9]

Can Dos

To ensure that pupils notice the progress they're making, and to celebrate it with them, at the end of each lesson Sarah asks her pupils to write down one thing that they can do as a result of that hour. As they leave the classroom, they tell Sarah what their 'Can Do' is that day. This is a quick, low-effort routine that concentrates pupils on their successes and builds up their sense that they can achieve and that they're making progress. It arose from Sarah's desire to build pupil confidence by 'celebrating success every lesson, rather than waiting for an assessment test success.'

I Can Wall

After a challenging first year in the classroom, confronting a great deal of negativity from pupils, Jessica knew that she 'wanted to have a massive emphasis on positivity' with her new class. She wanted to focus pupils on 'what they *can* do' and challenge their low expectations of themselves.

'I decided to create the I Can Wall at the very beginning of the year,' she says. 'I got every child to bring in a can and they all decorated them.' Jessica stuck the cans onto the wall and created a big display. Now whenever pupils succeed at something challenging, they write it down and put it into their can. The slips of paper mount up and, at regular points throughout the year, the class empty out their cans, share what they can do and celebrate together.

This simple strategy, Jessica says, was 'coupled with our class motto We Love Mistakes' (see p.71). 'Having these two running themes meant that if they faced something that was challenging, they would try and persist with that challenge, because they know that even if they do make mistakes at first, if they persevere they will learn from it. And then eventually that task, which they were finding really difficult, becomes something that they can do.'

Teaching pupils strategies to overcome challenges

- **Give pupils a simple framework to follow when they're stuck**
- **Teach pupils to select and use resources independently**
- **Teach pupils to manage impulses and deal with pressure**

A step on the way to independence is teaching pupils strategies for overcoming challenges on their own. 'Try to program scaffolds (e.g. hints, cues, prompts, additional research resources, or peers that help),' recommend Hattie and Yates, 'so that all learners feel able to move forwards in your classroom.'[10] By equipping pupils with methods for resolving their own problems they get into the habit of persisting with challenging work under their own steam. 'At the beginning of the year', Lowri says, 'if they couldn't do a piece of work they'd put it down and mess around. Now they know that it's a good thing that they're being challenged and they know what to do.'

Caveat: These scaffolds are not a substitute for dealing with deficits in essential subject knowledge. 'There are no shortcuts and no alternatives to trying to increase the factual knowledge that the child has not picked up', writes Daniel Willingham.[11]

Give pupils a simple framework to follow when they're stuck

A simple way of helping pupils to persist at challenging tasks is to ensure that they know what they can do when they get stuck. One way of doing this is to teach them a series of steps to follow that will help them to solve their problems. Darya, one of Lowri's pupils, gave me an example. 'We have this rule', she told me, 'and it's called "Stuck-in-the-Mud." If you get stuck:

- Read it again
- If you still don't understand then ask the person sitting by you
- If they don't understand, ask the whole table
- If they don't understand ask the teacher and then she'll teach it to all of us

Lowri also displays specific prompts and mnemonics around the classroom, which pupils can use to support themselves in different situations. "RUCSAC" is an aide memoire for how to solve maths problems, for example. 'We have a technique called "RUCSAC",' Akil told me, 'it means Read, then Understand, then Choose, then Solve, Answer, then Check to see.'

Learning Ladders

Each of Andreas's pupils has a laminated 'Learning Ladder' card next to them on their desk. It outlines a series of steps they can take if they're stuck on their work. 'They essentially have different things that they can do to climb the learning ladder,' says Andreas, 'with me at the top – I'm the last resort.' The steps on the ladder are as follows:

1   Stop and think! What do I already know?
2   Check the board and read the instructions
3   Would a dictionary or thesaurus help?
4   Ask your learning buddy. Can they help?
5   Be brave! Take a risk and have a go!
6   Ask an adult

Each card is lively, colourful and has the pupils name at the top, next to the words, 'Have you climbed the learning ladder?'

His pupil Nadeem described the value of this simple strategy: 'If we quickly ask the teacher what's the answer, Sir always tells us to go on the learning ladder and go on the steps. The first step is think about what should you do, then you look at the board, or ask a friend. It helps us a lot.' This resource simultaneously supports pupils to deal better with challenging situations and hands them the responsibility for doing so. Andreas introduced it in response to the huge number of 'comfort questions' he was receiving from pupils: questions and problems he was confident they could have resolved without him. Before he introduced the learning ladders, he asked an observer to count the number of comfort questions during an extended writing lesson; there were 44. Four months later, in an equivalent lesson, his observer only counted three. Reflecting on this tool, Andreas says that 'the ultimate goal must be for the learning ladder to disappear altogether but for the process it represents to remain in their minds.'

Teach pupils to select and use resources independently

Another way of getting pupils used to acting independently is to be less directive about exactly what classroom resources they should use and when. Instead, if basic resources are on hand, and pupils have been taught how to use them, they can get used to seeking them out as required. This is something that Andreas does as well as giving his students learning ladders; he makes resources available but doesn't prescribe exactly when or how to use them. As an English teacher, this includes dictionaries and thesauruses, as well as specific lesson resources and pupils' prior work. Although he doesn't tell pupils when to use what, he does give them frequent reminders, saying things like: 'The text is still there, you've got it in front of you', or 'if you're stuck, don't forget the list of ideas you've got in your book.' As with his learning ladders this is an interim step between dependence and independence: he is on standby, but expects pupils to take the initiative and help themselves. For another example see p.32.

Self-help cards

Patrick wanted his pupils to be equipped to deal with challenges independently, rather than giving up straight away or asking for help. One way he approached this was to make simple, relevant resources available to pupils at all times. He put sets of 'self-help cards' out onto the tables for different subjects. For example, 'for maths they have hundred squares and times tables,' he says, 'and they can choose those, and use them to help themselves, rather than coming to the teacher'. To embed this Patrick:

- Modelled how to use resources independently so that pupils had concrete examples to emulate
- Planned simple activities that require independence, and allowed pupils to use the available resources as they wished
- Prompted pupils to make the most of the resources when they asked for adult support
- Openly discussed and worked through frustrations with pupils if they struggled to adapt to this new way of working
- And celebrated pupil successes when they completed a challenging piece of work independently

---

Teach pupils to manage impulses and deal with pressure

'Self-control enables us to set priorities and resist impulsive actions or responses', in the words of Harvard's Center on the Developing Child.[12] It's essential for successful independent work, which requires pupils to stay focused and ignore tempting distractions, even when tasks are challenging. When it comes to developing self-control in the classroom, two complementary approaches are required:

1 Giving pupils structured opportunities to practise self-control
2 And limiting the amount of distractions and temptations in the classroom that require it

On the first point, Willingham suggests that things as simple as 'warmth, organization, and predictability' from the teacher can help pupils to get into the habit of acting in a self-controlled way:

> Children learn to self-regulate through practice. A well-organized classroom requires that children practice inhibiting their own moment-to moment desires in favor of acting in accordance with the pace set by the teacher.

To the second point, he adds that 'a well-organized classroom minimizes chaos and distractions'.[13] Duckworth, Gendler and Gross expand on this, suggesting that teachers should encourage pupils to seek out or create environments that will help them focus. '[M]anipulating our surroundings to advantage is, in fact, a highly effective form of self-control[14] [...] In self-control, the enemy is within', they write. 'Nevertheless, the most effective way to do battle with our inner demons may be, in fact, by taking the battle outside of the mind.'[15] As these remarks make clear, there is a balance to strike here: pupils need to practise showing self-control, but they should also, where possible, learn to avoid situations that require lots of it.

Here are some more specific methods for supporting the development of self-control, taken from the APA's 'Top 20 Principles from Psychology for Teaching and Learning' paper:

- 'Present the goals of lessons and tasks very clearly to students ... Break down tasks into smaller, "bitesize," meaningful components and clearly spell out the criteria for successful task performance.'
- Help pupils to 'identify and evaluate the short and long-term consequences of their decisions.'
- 'Use cues to alert students that important information is to follow when introducing a new concept to increase student attention.'
- Vary pace and intensity in lessons so that 'students are able to practice intense focusing followed by more socially interactive methods of learning.'[16]

Daniel Willingham notes that negative emotions reduce our ability to exercise self-control and advises that:

> When a student does act impulsively, a calm, warm correction and redirection of the student is more likely to prevent further impulsive acts than a rebuke that makes the student feel bad.

One lapse in self-control quickly catalyses others, unless pupils are supported to get back on track. Furthermore, Willingham states that 'teachers should expect that a student who is depressed or is having a hard time at home will have more difficulty working on his own, controlling his temper, and other tasks that require self-regulation.' Pupils experiencing external pressures 'might need more support from the environment – a quiet environment in which to work, for example, or more monitoring and guidance than other students on independent work.'[17]

Dweck, Walton and Cohen also accentuate the value of teaching pupils 'how to handle high pressure situations' – simple things like stopping and taking deep breaths, or visualising a safe place where you feel safe and in control.[18]

Case Study: Getting around the wall

When they struggled with a piece of work, Stephen's pupils would say 'I can't do it' and give up. 'There had been a lot of negativity around certain lessons', said Stephen, 'and there would be certain people saying *I can't do it, I can't do it . . . I can't draw* or *I can't do this skill.*' He decided that it would make a difference 'if the kids could conceptualise this *can't*' and knew 'what to do when they say they can't do something.' So to combat these negative attitudes and build a growth mindset, Stephen suggested that pupils visualise 'thinking you can't do something' as a wall, and then taught his class different strategies for 'getting around the wall' when they encounter it:

- He initially tackled the issue of pupils saying *I can't* in a standalone session. 'We put on a PowerPoint and we talked about things that we really struggle on or can't do', he said. Then 'I showed a picture of a wall, and a man looking over the wall, and lots of opportunities behind it.'
- Stephen related that image to the experience of struggling in the classroom and how, as soon as someone says *I can't do it* 'the wall goes up'. He asked the class how they could help themselves if they

felt like they couldn't do something. Some pupils 'said *Just say you can do it*', said Stephen. 'I said, *That's nice to say, but it doesn't always help.*'

- He and the class then brainstormed steps that pupils could take when they were struggling, including using a different resource, asking a friend and asking the teacher. Stephen's aim was to give 'the kids the opportunity to realise how they can actually overcome things.'
- 'The next day, as soon as someone said that they couldn't do something, I stopped the whole class', Stephen told me. 'I said *Look, what have we got here?* And someone said, *Well, Barney said he can't do it*, and I said *What does that mean?* Someone said, *That means he's never going to achieve anything in this lesson if he says that word.* By the end of the lesson, the class worked out solutions that Barney could do to help him improve.'
- The image of the wall became the basis of the way that Stephen's class talked about how to overcome challenges. In order to make this meaningful and effective he treated it like any other classroom routine, embedding and reinforcing it every day. 'To embed something like that', said Stephen, 'you have got to keep revisiting it. Now it's nice to see the class have got used to it, so when someone says that they can't, they say *He's got the wall, Sir, what can we do?*'

To support pupils when they're stuck, Stephen also created a display showing the steps that pupils can take if they're struggling. 'I just know that if I'm stuck', said Gill, 'that I can look through the other things I have done in my book and my next steps to try and improve. I can ask my partner for help, or if my partner was stuck they would ask me for help. If I got really stuck, and if I didn't understand it at all and if my partners didn't understand it at all, I would just go and ask.'

Enabling pupils to support, and seek support, from one another

- **Create an atmosphere of mutual support and responsibility**
- **Teach pupils to give one another feedback**

When pupils feel like they're part of a team, they are more likely to take risks and make an effort. At best, a class of pupils can become a powerful mutual support network: developing ideas together; offering mutual assistance when they're struggling; acting as examples for one another; and, perhaps most powerfully, providing one another with feedback. Dweck, Walton and Cohen write that building a strong group dynamic and identity can help pupils 'learn not only that they will reach a higher standard, but also that they will help their classmates as a group to do so.' The experience of 'working with others', they continue, 'helps students to enjoy, value, and work hard on challenging tasks.'[19]

Becky's pupils describe the value of completing tasks in pairs. 'When we have paired work,' says Jane, 'you are working together to come up with a complete answer, which you both have put work into. It's usually a good answer because you have different knowledge you can put together to create the solution to the problem.' 'Often you are purposely paired with people at different levels', says Rose, 'and you might be more knowledgeable in an area, but your partner might also be knowledgeable in another area and you can combine the skills and get a better answer.' 'It's not just being taught by the teacher,' says Jane, 'other people can teach you – which makes things easier to know because you get to learn it from a pupil's perspective.'

Create an atmosphere of mutual support and responsibility

When pupils know that the objective is to support one another, and not to compete with one another, they are far more likely to focus on making progress as a group and not on appearing more successful than their peers. Where competition can be healthy and motivating, the 'Top 20 Principles from Psychology' paper suggests, is having 'teams of mixed ability groups that compete with each other to reach a common goal.'[20] Dweck, Walton and Cohen echo and expand on this idea, stating that pupils 'are often more motivated and successful when classroom activities involve cooperative rather than competitive or individualistic goals.'[21]

As well as explicitly talking to your pupils about what a brilliant support network they can be for one another (something we saw on p.32), the simplest way for teachers to build an atmosphere of mutual support is to give pupils tasks that require collaboration, and to establish clear expectations so that each person's input is valued. When group work is effective, write Dweck, Walton and Cohen, 'each group member enacts competence and contributes to the group.'[22]

'They sit in a team on their table and they know that they are responsible for making sure everyone understands,' says Sam about her pupils. 'They are more than happy to help each other and to accept help; they are happy to say, *I'm not sure* to their partner, *can you help me?* At first we struggled a little bit and they would be*: No, I can do it, I don't want your help.* Especially the boys: *No, I don't need your help, I can do it.* But now they have realised it's actually not a bad thing to say: *Please can you help me, I'm a bit stuck.*'

See p.89 for a group work case study and, for an example of effective pair work, see p.25.

Passing questions from group to group

Sarah splits her class into groups and asks each group to work on a different question. 'Once you've picked apart your question in your group,' she says, 'you're then going to pass that question on to another group and they're going to have another go at it as well.' Each group looks at each of the questions and adds to the previous groups' ideas. Sarah does this, she tells pupils, to 'pull together all of our brain power, all of our analysis skills'.

Pupil teachers

'We do this pupil-teacher thing,' says Dana, one of Hayley's science pupils, 'where one of us will go up and be the teacher for part of a lesson and we learn things and it's fun.' For ten minutes of every lesson, Hayley hands over the reins to one of her pupils, who is tasked to teach a new concept to the class. The pupil-teacher prepares their micro-lesson in advance. After they teach it, Hayley reinforces the concept that they've introduced over the rest of the lesson.

This activity both depends on, and develops, a collaborative classroom culture. It builds confidence, as pupils stand up in an expert capacity, and independence as pupils are given a greater role in their own and their peers' learning. 'It's weird but fun', Dana continues, 'because they are teaching us and they ask us stuff . . . I think it boosts confidence and what you know at the same time.'

Teach pupils to give one another feedback

What 'teachers routinely report', writes Dylan Wiliam, 'is that students tend to be much tougher on one another than most teachers would dare to be. This is important because it suggests that with well-structured peer-assessment, one can achieve better outcomes than would be possible with one adult for every student.'[23] This is a tantalising thought and suggests that teachers have a huge resource right under their noses if they create opportunities for pupils to give one another feedback.

For peer-assessment to be meaningful, however, pupils need to be taught how to do it. If they dive into it without guidance you face some of the following risks:

- Pupils not knowing enough about a topic to provide useful, or even correct, feedback
- Pupils providing vague, confusing or superficial feedback
- Pupils withholding useful feedback to avoid hurting one another's feelings or, on the other hand, offering feedback in a negative way that deflates confidence

As these points imply, peer-assessment can be ineffective, and even counter-productive, if it's not set up properly. To teach pupils to do it effectively:

1 Begin by brainstorming the potential value, and the potential pitfalls, of peer-assessment. Ask pupils to generate a list of benefits and risks.
2 Talk about the potential discomfort of hearing critical comments from peers. The Deans for Impact 'Science of Learning' report suggests that teachers should 'encourage students to see critical feedback as a sign of others' beliefs that they are able to meet high standards.'[24]
3 Discuss how feedback can be delivered in the most useful way, coming up with examples of phrases that pupils could use. Discuss both the need for frankness, and the need to be constructive. Phrases that pupils suggest could be collected and displayed in the classroom for future reference.

4   Practise doing this as a whole class to begin with, perhaps projecting a piece of work or handing out photocopies. Go through the whole process together, with you modelling what to do and talking your thoughts aloud.

5   Ensure that peer-assessment always has a very specific aim, so that pupils know exactly what they're looking for or commenting on. Give pupils success criteria or examples to guide them where necessary.

6   Agree in advance on the format that feedback will take, perhaps giving pupils a model or framework to follow.

7   After each peer-assessment session, review how it went. Discuss examples of the feedback that pupils gave and received, and how it could be even more useful next time.

8   Until pupils have become adept at giving one another feedback, begin each peer-assessment session by revisiting the principles of how to give effective feedback and by modelling exactly what you're expecting from pupils.

Dylan Wiliam is emphatic about the advantages of using peer-assessment. First, 'we are all better at spotting mistakes in the work of others than we are in our own work. Second, when we notice mistakes in the work of others, we are less likely to make the same mistakes in our own work.'[25]

Peer marking

To encourage a trusting collaborative culture, Sarah asks her pupils to assess one another's written work. She gives them very specific success criteria to tick off as they read through work by a peer. She then asks them to 'put a comment – something you like about it – and a target – something that needs to be improved'. In the process, pupils receive valuable feedback, get used to supporting one another, and think analytically about what success looks like and how to achieve it.

Similarly, Thomas sometimes asks his pupils to read and provide feedback on an anonymised piece of work by a peer, using a marking scheme he provides for them. 'One person in here has had their work photocopied. It's unmarked', he said in a lesson I observed. 'Read through this and annotate it. You're going to be a teacher. You're going to annotate what you like about this and what you want to improve.' Thomas then asked everyone to 'write two things this pupil does well and two things they could do to improve their paragraph.' This sharpens pupils' awareness of what success looks like, provides them with insights they can use to improve their own work, and enables them to practise assessing work by peers in a structured, whole-class situation. Dedicating time to analysing a piece of work and considering how it could be improved also foregrounds the value of feedback, the idea that each piece of work can yield information that pupils can use to improve the next. For another example of peer marking see p.33 and for an example of pupils giving one another other verbal feedback see p.33.

Punctuation Patrol Officers

During independent writing tasks, James E allocates two Punctuation Patrol Officers (PPOs) to wear a fireman's helmet and patrol the classroom checking other pupils' work for missing capital letters and full stops, or for other easy-to-spot, frequently made errors. They use a special pen to correct their classmates' work.

Case Study: Talk Triangles

'I'm exciting, but I'm not that exciting', says Elizabeth, remarking on how well her pupils can support and learn from one another. 'So I formed Talk Triangles, with a lead pupil and two other pupils that feed into it. The lead pupils are like mini teachers.' Talk Triangles provide a simple structure for group discussions and function as follows:

- Elizabeth puts pupils into mixed ability groups of three;
- She allocates a lead pupil, who guides their group through a series of questions
- The three pupils support one another as they answer

To make these conversations effective, Elizabeth does the following each time she uses it:

- She describes what pupils need to do in minute detail
- She models the routine so that pupils can see a real life example of exactly what's expected of them. With her teaching assistants or two

pupils she role-plays the group activity that pupils are about to do. Even though they regularly use this Talk Triangle routine, Elizabeth models the specific task every time.

- While modelling, she explicitly describes the characteristics of good group work, stating, for example, 'I'm watching for the children who are most careful to make sure that everybody gets a go' and 'I'm watching for the people who still turn their faces to look at the other people once they've had a go'.
- She provides written question prompts. Lead pupils use these as a structure for the group conversations.
- At the end of each discussion in Talk Triangles, Elizabeth asks pupils to assess how well they worked in a group. Pupils discuss this among themselves and then Elizabeth leads a short whole-class conversation about effective group work, with pupils feeding in what did and didn't go well in their Talk Triangles.
- Finally, Elizabeth uses the routine regularly so that it becomes part of classroom life

The Talk Triangles increase pupils' responsibility for aspects of their own, and their classmates', learning and provide a safe space for pupils to take risks and make mistakes.

Demanding maximum effort and quality from pupils

- Inject pace and urgency into lessons
- Have exacting standards of behaviour and personal organisation
- Expect pupils' best effort and participation
- Create an academic atmosphere in the classroom

All pupils need to be pushed and to feel the force of their teachers' high expectations for them: to encounter in the classroom what Ron Berger calls an 'ethic and culture that compels students to achieve more than they think possible.'[26] The level and intensity of the challenges we present pupils with sends an implicit message about how we see them and what we think they're capable of. What 'actually communicates expectations to students is teacher behavior', writes Robert Marzano. 'Students for whom teachers have low expectations', he continues, 'become accustomed to the teacher asking them fewer and less challenging questions than other students.'[27]

'She makes people work as hard as they possibly can', says Karim about Becky. 'Not in a mean way – she inspires them to work hard . . . She has really high expectations of us and, whenever we achieve them, she praises us.'

Inject pace and urgency into lessons

One way to communicate high expectations is to ensure that there's a mood of urgency in your classroom – challenging pupils from the moment they walk through the door and teaching purposeful, fast-paced lessons. 'The achievement gap is pretty much a practice gap', thinks Mark. As such, he wants his pupils to use every lesson to best effect. 'Every single lesson when they come in, there's work that they have to do straight away and they are pushed to use every minute that they've got.' His explicit message to pupils every lesson is: '*It's really, really important that you learn today.*' This hits home, he says, through 'repetition and genuinely meaning it'.

One of James S's pupils described the way he pushes them to take responsibility for their own work. 'He's a friendly teacher, but he doesn't beat around the bush. We are in Year 11 now and a lot of the work is up to us. And he's like: *If you don't do this, if YOU don't do this, you're not going to succeed.* He doesn't dress that up for us because that's just how it is.'

Do Now

Having a 'Do Now' task prepared for pupils when they arrive in the classroom is a simple and common routine, but for Chris it's a potent way of 'not allowing any dead time in the classroom' and communicating his belief and determination that they will succeed. For Chris the 'Do Now' needs to be a solo task that focuses pupils: 'a challenge, a game, it could simply be *Come in and read your book*.' 'You have to craft these tasks so they're black and white,' he cautions. 'An awful task would be *Discuss with your friend what happened last lesson*. It needs to be something that gets them to come in and get on with their work diligently.'

Have exacting standards of behaviour and personal organisation

The tiny details of pupils' behaviour and personal organisation contribute to how well they do academically. As such, it's crucial to hold pupils to very high standards in both areas. 'It's the small details that make up the bigger picture; the small things that might seem pedantic', says Chris, explaining his insistence on pupils 'arriving to the lesson organised, with their equipment, wearing the uniform correctly, having done the work expected of them' and on pupils presenting work smartly and 'expressing themselves clearly in full sentences'. He also has very clear routines and procedures around entering the classroom and other transitions, routines that he established through 'repetition and practising' at the beginning of the year. 'A lot of kids come from very chaotic backgrounds', he told me, and appreciate the order and consistency of his classroom. In his opinion, 'structure liberates learning'. Basic habits of organisation and behaviour provide a foundation on which good academic habits can be built.

Expect pupils' best effort and participation

Pupils need to know that you will only accept their best efforts and that they can't get away with anything less. 'Holding students to high standards and giving them the attention and scaffolding they need to meet those standards sends the message of personal concern', write Dweck, Walton and Cohen. 'In a sense, good teachers are like good parents – at times authoritative but consistently caring.'[28]

This doesn't mean that everything pupils do needs to be perfect, but that you're expecting full engagement and their best attempt at all times. '*I'm not going to do it, because I'm not very good at it and there is no point in me trying because I'm not going to get anywhere with it*', Charlie recalls one of his pupils saying to him. Consequently, 'one of the rules in my classes', he says, 'is that I don't mind if you get it wrong as long as you try ... If they try something and get it wrong there is never going to be a problem as long as they have put the effort in in the first place.'

Similarly, Rebecca doesn't accept work unless she believes it's the best her pupils can do. 'We have a kind of *Try, try, try again* message,' she says. If she believes a pupil has dashed off a piece of work that doesn't represent what they're capable of, she'll tell them: 'You're going to have to do it in your break time' or 'That will be done in your own time, because that's not good enough.' 'I have been really firm with that,' she says, 'and it's starting to show benefits. At the beginning of the year, I had children repeat work twice or maybe three times until they had a piece of good work that they were proud of and I was proud of.' To ensure that this is a positive, not punitive, process, she emphasises how proud she is of their completed work, and how proud they should be, and sends them to show finished pieces to other adults as well. Setting this standard has led her pupils to raise their expectations of themselves. 'Just the other day', says Rebecca, 'a girl in my class started a piece of work and, without me even saying anything to her, she came up to me and said, *I'm not happy with this, Miss. Can I do it again?* And she started the whole piece again of her own accord. She didn't have to be told that it wasn't good enough, she just did it again, which I thought was great.' See p.98 and p.100 for case studies on expecting effort and participation in whole-class discussions.

Create an academic atmosphere in the classroom

All classrooms focus on academic work, but they don't necessarily *feel* academic and scholarly. Crafting this kind of atmosphere, by modelling your own enthusiasm for a subject, or by giving pupils a taste of more advanced content or ways of working, is another way of demonstrating your belief in your pupils' abilities and your expectation that they will engage with work in a concerted, scholarly manner.

When I spoke to Rose, in Becky's Year 9 maths class, she expressed pride at the advanced academic material that Becky sometimes drops into her lessons. 'She will add in little bits that may not necessarily be connected to the lesson – well, they will be but they will be on a much, much higher level; for example, she might include a bit of A Level stuff.' Becky selects advanced details, which pupils don't need to know but might find thought-provoking, and peppers them into her lessons from time-to-time, making it explicit to pupils when she does so.

'People kept saying: *Oh, it's really academic in here*', said Joe about visitors to his classroom. He explained why: 'I look at these Year 9s and I think *What do they need to do to sit the A Level and why are they not doing those things now?* They can do it if you tell them they can do it and they believe they can do it.' As such, he tries 'to make every class an A Level style environment – so they can succeed, so there's no jump up, no surprises.' He does this through the way he talks to pupils, the way he organises discussions, the skills he tries to develop, and the range of materials he refers to. I heard something similar from Dan. 'I consciously expose my Year 11s to very academic material,' he told me, 'and I make it very explicit to them that this is university level material because then they don't have that sense of intimidation. Perhaps in the future when they go off to colleges or when they apply for university, they'll have a sense that *I belong here and this is an environment that I'm comfortable with.*' For a teacher consciously using academic language with pupils see p.26.

Case Study: Expecting participation in whole-class discussions

Cold-calling

Lawrence explicitly focuses on 'teaching [pupils] how to be confident'. Specifically, he wants them to feel comfortable speaking out and articulating themselves even when they're uncertain of a response. One way he does this is to call on people at random rather than asking for hands up to answer questions. Lawrence uses the well-known lolly stick approach: he has a tin of lolly sticks, each of which has a pupil's name written on it; whenever he has a question for the class, he draws a stick at random and pupils know that they can be called on at any time. Lawrence explains to pupils that he is using this strategy because:

- He wants to hear from all of them
- He values effort and thoughtful participation, not just correct answers
- He wants them to be comfortable and confident expressing themselves

This explanation isn't a one-off occurrence. Lawrence regularly returns to these ideas so that the intention of the routine isn't forgotten. By combining this common cold-calling technique with an explicit, encouraging message, he tries to 'generate a degree of comfort through naturalisation'. He wants pupils to 'get used to the process of talking and sometimes not being completely right'.

Thinking space

When calling on pupils at random, there will inevitably be moments when someone dries up and simply doesn't know what to say. Being exposed like this can be an uncomfortable knock to confidence and Lawrence uses a simple strategy to counter this risk. 'If they can't give the answer,' he says, 'I'll ask somebody to help them and tell them I'll come back to them.'

'I'll come back to you', is the kind of thing it's very easy to say and then forget to do. In fact, it can easily become a euphemistic way of saying '*You failed this time, but don't worry about it*'. When somebody stumbles, Lawrence calls on their peers for input and commits to coming back to them. By the time he does, they've formulated a response and end the interaction feeling supported and successful.

Almost, not quite, not yet

Lawrence chooses his words carefully while leading whole-class discussions: he's enthusiastic about pupil responses, but doesn't devalue his praise by suggesting that everything is correct and equally insightful. 'I try to disabuse them of the notion that English is the subject where there is no wrong answer', he says, 'because that also leads to them thinking, *Well, what's the point?* I tell them there are degrees of rightness, if you like.' As such, he uses expressions like 'almost', 'not quite' and 'not yet' a great deal, while simultaneously sharpening his questions and pushing pupils to be more precise.

When we spoke to one of Lawrence's pupils at the end of the year, she described the change in her attitude after a year in his class: 'We've become more confident – even generally as a person, more confident to actually express ourselves. It sounds so clichéd, but it's actually true, because before I was like . . . I never wanted to say something if I didn't know if it was correct or not. Now, I'll just say it. It might be wrong, it might be insightful . . . I can learn from it anyway. He's taught me that.'

Case Study: Class debates

'They plan to say the minimum answer that they can give, the most basic answer', said Susannah, describing the way pupils were participating in her RE lessons. This challenge – low participation, born of low confidence – led her to develop new routines for whole-class discussions, which would make pupils more comfortable airing views and being challenged. Now she holds lively whole-class debates, within the following parameters:

Framing discussions as debates

Susannah frames whole-class discussions as a debate in which pupils can air an assortment of differing views. She stresses that she's looking for a variety of perspectives and normalises the idea that pupils' responses will be challenged by the teacher and their peers.

Cold-calling

She expects all pupils to be ready to participate. 'Miss gives us the chance to put our hands up and disagree or not, but most of the time she just picks on us', said one pupil. Everyone knows that they could be called on at any time.

Bouncing questions around the room

Pupils are expected to respond to one another's views, not simply to contribute their own ideas. 'I try and bounce questions around the room as much as I can' she says, 'which means that they have to be on it, because if you say, *Why do you agree? Why do you disagree?* they have to remember what the other person said.'

Asking open questions

Susannah constantly asks open questions to push for further detail. 'She literally interrogates pupils,' a colleague told us, 'which is brilliant. It sounds bad, but it's not. Pupils are there to be interrogated: to get the best out of them, to know what they understand, and to really push them in their learning.'

Encouraging respectful disagreement

Susannah encourages pupils to challenge one another's perspectives, but she has two routines to ensure that these interactions are respectful and constructive. 'You can disagree with someone quite frankly and openly, but you have to do it in a polite way,' she says.

- Pupils have to start their sentence with a structure like 'I agree because...' or 'I disagree because...' Before embedding this habit, Susannah sometimes heard remarks like 'You're wrong' or 'That's rubbish'.
- They also have to use one another's names in their responses. This immediately makes discussions feel more respectful and now, with practice, pupils stop and correct themselves if they forget.

These whole-class debates provide a safe space for pupils to experience being pushed and challenged by the teacher and their peers, build confidence in expressing themselves and become more open to feedback.

Providing pupils with opportunities to work independently

- Give pupils structured periods of independence
- Make homework as meaningful as possible
- Teach pupils to practise effectively

Although it's crucial to expect and demand the best from pupils, our ultimate aim is that they demand the best from themselves. There's a delicate balance to be struck in the classroom, therefore, between supporting pupils, pushing pupils and stepping aside so that pupils have opportunities to push themselves and overcome their own challenges. Katie's hope for her classroom is that 'instead of me being in the middle of the class with them all around me doing what I say, I'm standing on the outside of the class – very much in the room – but standing on the outside of the class with them independently learning and really motivated to do it for themselves.' John Hattie expresses the power of pupil autonomy as follows: 'the greatest effects on pupil learning occur when teachers become learners of their own teaching, and when pupils become their own teachers.'[29] To do this, pupils need opportunities to attempt difficult work independently.

Give pupils structured periods of independence

Having explored ways of supporting children to overcome their own challenges on p.83, here the emphasis is on providing pupils with specific tasks and blocks of time in which they can practise working independently and put the extra prompts or resources you've given them to use. William James described the powerful effect that these moments of struggling and autonomously overcoming difficulty can have on pupils: 'A victory scored under such conditions becomes a turning-point [...]', he wrote, 'and serves thereafter as an ideal pattern for self-imitation.'[30]

Open-ended questions

Many of Becky's Year 7 maths pupils arrived from primary school with a negative attitude towards maths and give up straight away if something is difficult. To encourage them to have a go and give them a sense of achievement, Becky frequently sets open-ended investigations without a single right answer. 'I'll give them a question,' says Becky, 'and ask them to think about how many solutions they can get.' Open-ended tasks, which all pupils can attempt at their own level, remove the risk of failure and get pupils accustomed to having a go at a subject they're uncomfortable with. Pupils can stretch themselves as much as they want and feel a sense of achievement for the solutions they come up with.

Giving pupils freedom to decide how they'll approach a task

Andreas often refrains from telling pupils exactly how they ought to approach independent tasks and, instead, gives them the freedom to select from a range of options. As he introduces an activity based on a text, for example, he says 'Maybe read it again; maybe you don't need to; maybe discuss it with the person next to you' and reminds pupils that they can make use of their learning ladders (see p.79), their prior work and other resources that are at their disposal around the classroom. Pupils are expected to navigate challenges and complete work to a high standard, but they aren't compelled to do so in one specific way.

Stock phrases

To encourage her pupils to overcome challenges independently, Ally uses two simple stock phrases – 'You need to find a solution to your problem' and 'What are you going to do?' – when they approach her for support with issues she knows they could resolve themselves.

Make homework as meaningful as possible

Homework can be a good opportunity to practise completing challenging work without a teacher's support. To make the most of this opportunity, it needs to be as meaningful as possible, and not something that can be ignored or dashed off.

Valuing homework

To improve the quality of the work pupils did at home, Thomas took the following steps:

Giving pupils a tight turnaround: 'He will set you homework on Tuesday and he would want it back by Thursday,' said one pupil. 'He wants us to do it early and to do it quick – to remember everything that we did in the lesson.'

Marking it immediately: For pupils, the fact that Thomas wants homework back so quickly and then marks it quickly shows that 'he really cares'.

Taking time in lessons to review and learn from it: When he returns homework, Thomas runs a Learning Response lesson, in which pupils respond to his feedback and improve their work.

Expecting homework to be completed promptly to a high standard, demonstrates his high expectations to pupils and pushes their independence: they need to be well organised and they know that the quality of the work they do will affect the benefit they get from Thomas' feedback.

Pre-work

Frustrated that she was always chasing her pupils for their homework, Lucy restructured her lessons so that they had to prepare for each lesson at home, instead of doing homework based on the previous lesson. 'The lesson's going to be on this: I want you to find out these things,' she would tell pupils, and they would have to come to the next lesson fully prepared.

To ease the transition to this new way of working, Lucy involved the parents. She sat down with pupils and their parents at a parents' evening and asked her pupils 'Where are you now?' and 'Where do you want to be?' Once she'd discussed their ambitions she said, 'Right, well how are we going to get there then?' She made a list of actions with pupils and parents, emphasising the importance of working at home. 'The parents got on board with it as well', she says. 'So it was more than just me and the classroom. It was like, not a formal home–school agreement, but a mutual: *We're going to work as a team all together.*'

Expecting pupils to have studied prior to the lesson made homework a more urgent matter. 'Before', Lucy says, her pupils' attitude to their learning 'was more *it's the teacher's job* and afterwards, it was very much like: *It's my responsibility. My teacher helps me, but it's my responsibility.*'

Teach pupils to practise effectively

It's one thing getting pupils to work with greater focus and independence, it's another thing supporting them to make the very most of their time. As Daniel Willingham writes, '[e]xperience means you are simply engaged in the activity. Practice means you are trying to improve your performance.'[31] Pupils need to know how to practise effectively and need the motivation to do the focused, sometimes gruelling, work that deliberate practice entails. In John Hattie's words, 'how we teach kids to enjoy the practice is the art of learning'.[32]

The kind of deliberate practice that accelerates learning is not mere repetition. It requires, writes Angela Duckworth:

- 'A clearly defined stretch goal
- Full concentration and effort
- Immediate and informative feedback
- Repetition with reflection and refinement'

Although, in her words, '[e]ach of the basic requirements of deliberate practice is unremarkable', the combined effect of pupils being out of their comfort zone, committing full attention to a specific skill, or aspect of a skill, then receiving and responding to high quality feedback, is extremely powerful.[33]

The first step in teaching pupils this kind of practice is to talk to them about it, discussing the steps involved, asking them whether they can think of times when they've engaged in this kind of intensive improvement before, and describing your own experiences. An important point to discuss is how uncomfortable and tiring this kind of practice can be, due to the fact that you're working at the very edge of your current capabilities. Once pupils are familiar with the theory behind deliberate practice, they need to experience it. Some key points for the teacher here are:

- Ensure that pupils are practising a very specific skill, or part of a skill
- Show pupils an example of exactly what success looks like beforehand
- Hold back and give pupils space to struggle and persevere
- Encourage pupils but be wary of offering empty praise before they've made progress
- Be on hand with feedback as pupils make mistakes

The nature of this kind of practice – working on a very specific outcome – means, writes Daisy Christodoulou, 'that lessons may look very different from the final skill they are hoping to instil.'[34]

Enabling pupils to monitor and direct their own progress

- Give pupils an active role in monitoring their progress
- Allow pupils to select and adjust the level of challenge
- Teach pupils to plan out work and set goals for themselves

The best way to genuinely hand pupils ownership of their learning, and help them to connect day-to-day work to longer term hopes, is to enable them to keep track of their own progress, set themselves goals, and plan out their own work. Being able to monitor how they're doing and plan out where they're going next gives pupils a sense of control and autonomy and, ultimately, allows them to take greater responsibility for their own achievement. As Dylan Wiliam writes, 'activating students as owners of their own learning can produce extraordinary improvements in their achievement'.[35]

According to Deci and Ryan's 'self-determination theory', intrinsic motivation is a product of feeling autonomous, competent, and feeling that you have strong personal connections. Feeling connected to others featured heavily in the sections of this guide to do with building relationships and building a sense of team; making pupils feel competent has cropped up throughout this guide, notably in sections on enabling pupils to experience success and to notice the progress they are making. These final sections on giving pupils the opportunity to work independently and to monitor and direct their own progress are directed squarely at building pupils' sense of their autonomy and ownership of their learning.

Dan told me that he wants his pupils to 'move beyond the idea that education is something that happens to you'. Likewise, Hattie and Yates write that 'learning is optimised when teachers see learning through the eyes of the learner, and when learners see themselves as their own teachers.'[36] This is not an invitation for the teacher to opt-out or stop leading instruction, but rather a point about perceptions: particularly, about pupils feeling that they have an active, in fact leading, role in their own learning and success.

Give pupils an active role in monitoring their progress

Handing pupils responsibility for monitoring and directing their own progress – by teaching them to assess their own work and set themselves goals – is one of the most powerful ways to develop genuine independence and put their learning into their hands. As Dylan Wiliam writes: assessment isn't first and foremost about monitoring pupils, it's 'about pupils becoming owners of their own learning.'[37] There is a spectrum of activity that you can engage in here, as the examples in this section demonstrate. Self-assessment can involve anything from simple, well-known measures like giving pupils red, amber and green discs so that they can communicate their level of understanding to the teacher throughout the lesson, or asking pupils to draw a red, amber or green traffic light at the end of a piece of work, to pupils filling out a 'learning log' at the end of a lesson, or looking critically at a piece of their work and using a rubric to identify strengths and areas for improvement.

It takes time to teach pupils to effectively assess their own work. As Wiliam writes elsewhere: '[m]any teachers have found that students' first attempts at self-assessment are usually neither insightful nor useful.'[38] This is not only because pupils need to learn new skills, it's also because '[r]eflecting on learning is emotionally charged,' Wiliam continues, 'which is why developing such skills takes time, especially with students who are accustomed to failure.'[39] As such, the principle value of self-assessment is its impact on pupils – helping them reflect on, and take ownership of, their learning – rather than its accuracy; self-reported information is not a substitute for your own assessment of pupil learning.

Caveat: A crucial first step in self-assessment is ensuring that pupils have a clear vision of what success looks like. Dylan Wiliam advises that teachers '[s]tart with samples of work, rather than rubrics, to communicate quality'. Rubrics – lists of the expectations for different levels of achievement – can be valuable tools for empowering pupils. But, Wiliam warns, they 'are best regarded as the culmination of a developmental process that begins with examination of samples of students' work. So, before your students do a laboratory report, before they write a ghost story, spend some time getting them to look at other students' attempts at similar tasks.' In other words, instead of beginning with technical lists of expectations, give pupils the opportunity to scrutinise excellent examples of work by others. To encourage pupils to look at this critically, you could ask them to brainstorm their own list of success criteria based on the models you provided.

Coded marking

Instead of correcting pupils' basic punctuation and spelling mistakes when he's marking, Andreas expects them to correct their own work based on a system of coded marking. It works as follows:

- Andreas highlights each mistake and writes a number next to it. The number corresponds to a simple list of different types of error.
- Pupils have time in lessons to respond to his marking. They match the numbers to the type of error on the list.
- As far as possible, pupils correct their own mistakes, using dictionaries or other resources as appropriate.
- They then rewrite the paragraph that contains the most errors.

'You've got immediate progress', Andreas explains. 'The errors have gone down and then you're able to mark it again with the same codes' and show pupils the progress they've made. From Andreas's perspective, it also means that his marking takes 'a third of the time it did before.'

Self-testing

Lian uses self-testing to enable pupils to track their own progress more effectively. For example, when asking the children to check whether they've remembered the method for solving a new type of maths problem, she 'would teach the children explicitly how to check whether they have committed a method to memory', she told me, either 'by having examples of the method written out that children can cover and then check' or by 'giving them additional questions with the answers and then getting them to see if they can get the answers correctly themselves.' Lian also described how she would also use self-testing more broadly, using a blank timetable as a kind of learning log with pupils: 'At the end of the day, I would give them a timetable and get them to write down the key learning from each lesson.'

Self Audit

Thomas periodically asks pupils to evaluate their strengths and areas for development against a rubric of requirements for GCSE English. To do this:

- He gives pupils a 'Self-Audit' template, which lists the key criteria.
- He asks pupils to colour-code their responses with highlighters, checking each point against their most recent pieces of written work. They use green for aspects they 'do well or do all of the time', yellow for things they 'sometimes do and sometimes forget' and pink for things they 'don't do or don't do well'.
- Before they begin, Thomas models filling in the audit: 'It says *I write the question down that I am answering.* I highlight green – yes I do that. *I make a minimum of three points of analysis* – hmm, I sometimes do this, so it's a maybe.'

By asking pupils to identify their own strengths and areas to develop, Thomas sends the message that they need to take responsibility for their own learning. It builds confidence as pupils see the areas where they are performing strongly – and see improvement from one 'Self-Audit' to the next – and gives pupils the information they need to progress further.

Allow pupils to select and adjust the level of challenge

Within a classroom with high expectations, presenting pupils with tasks of varying difficulty and allowing them to select the level of challenge to attempt can be a good way of handing them greater ownership of their learning. This means that struggling or under-confident pupils can begin on work they can definitely succeed at, but aren't limited to it, and all pupils can independently stretch themselves, building confidence by achieving more than they expected. Some caution is required with this technique, particularly on first introducing it, and you may need to intervene if pupils select work that is clearly far too easy or difficult.

Letting pupils choose the difficulty level

In her maths lessons, Lucy sets a range of tasks at different difficulty levels, without specifying who should do what. Outlining the choices in one lesson, Lucy says:

> I've got these sheets here – these are sheets that are just going to take you through it step-by-step: what you need to do first, then a bit more difficult, and a bit more difficult . . . If you're thinking *I'm just not getting it*.

> Then I've got some grade B and some grade A work – the answers are on the back so you can check if you're getting it right.

> Last but not least, these are the really difficult ones, the grade A* ones.

She invites pupils to 'come up and get what you want', offering an exam question as a warm up too. Lucy allocates different tables to the different levels of challenge and pupils move around the classroom freely, working with others as they wish. 'You've got your friends to do it with as well,' says Jenny, 'so if you can't do something, you ask the person next to you.'

This system simultaneously offers pupils a safety net and the opportunity to push themselves as far and as fast as they want. 'You do your own level of work,' says Jenny, 'so it's not like you're forced to do anything: you do what you want to do.' 'We do it quite a lot,' says Alex. 'It's so that we can decide what level we are at – because she knows we're mature enough to actually know which one we're going for.' For Alex, it means that 'you know that you're kind of in control of your learning.'

This method makes progression tangible for pupils: they can see exactly what's required at each level and what they need to do to advance. 'If you're working at a B,' says one of her pupils, 'you can push yourself and try the A ones. I try to push myself to do more and I try different things.' For other examples of teachers allowing pupils to choose the level of challenge see p.27 and p.31.

Teach pupils to plan out work and set goals for themselves

The 'Top 20 Principles from Psychology' paper states that pupils 'with a goal and adequate self-efficacy are likely to engage in the activities that lead to attainment of that goal. Self-efficacy is also increased as students monitor the progress they are making toward their goals, especially when they are acquiring new skills in the process.' To get pupils into the habit of setting goals and working towards them, they recommend that they keep 'a written record of goal progress that is regularly checked by both the student and the teacher'.[40]

Kayleigh's pupils routinely set themselves three targets after she hands back pieces of marked work and then refer to these targets while working on their next assignment (see p.31 for more detail). Kayleigh sees the ability to set targets and monitor your own progress as a fundamental skill, which pupils can use in all areas of their education. She gives the example of one pupil who was preparing for a speaking exam: 'She came to me at break time in the playground and she had a little notebook, and she said *Miss, these are my targets for my learning assessment: I need to do this, I need to do this, and I need to do this, and check them off as I do them.* And I was laughing, because I'd created a monster.' 'They are taking these skills away and applying them elsewhere,' says Kayleigh, 'and I think that's great.'

Before we ask pupils to set themselves goals, however, we need to make sure that we've taught them how to do it and provided them with clear examples. The key step here is to model how to write a SMART (Specific, Measurable, Attainable, Relevant, Time-limited) goal – beginning with a woolly ambition and sharpening it, with pupils' support, into a clear, concrete objective. Once pupils have seen you modelling the process, they then need the opportunity to draft goals for themselves. To begin with, they could practise coming up with goals related to a personal interest, and then you could ask them to apply the same process to a specific academic target.

You might then ask pupils to keep 'a written record of goal progress', as suggested above. Whichever way you ask pupils to record their goals, the best moment to ask pupils to set them is after you, their peers, or they themselves have assessed a piece of work. The knowledge from the assessment of what's going well and what needs to be improved can then feed directly into pupils' goal setting, giving them a very clear sense of what they need to tackle next. Depending on your pupils' comfort with this process, you could provide them with a template or simple sentence starters to support them.

Once pupils have got the hang of setting SMART goals based on feedback, it simply becomes a routine part of classroom life. The level of scaffolding and the complexity of the goals will vary across the age range, but the process is the same regardless. Nevertheless, asking pupils to set themselves goals can sound daunting at first, to teachers and pupils, and it can feel more secure to retain control of this process yourself. Dweck, Walton and Cohen remark on this common habit in teachers:

> [T]eachers sometimes unnecessarily constrain student autonomy by giving continual commands; providing solutions before the student has had an opportunity to solve a problem independently; limiting choices for reading and writing exercises; and dispensing unnecessary incentives like gold stars, rewards, and bribes for good work, such as extra recess time. It's important to note that autonomy-supportive classrooms are not laissez-faire. Instead, they structure activities in a way that advances concrete goals for learning but that simultaneously encourages students to see themselves as agents in their own growth.[41]

Letting pupils behind the scenes so that they know where learning is going, can monitor their progress, and then set themselves goals, using success criteria, marking schemes, or your feedback, is a powerful way of handing them greater autonomy.

Notes

1   Dweck, C., Walton, G., and Cohen, G. (2011). *Academic Tenacity: Mindsets and Skills that Promote Long-Term Learning.* Seattle, WA: The Gates Foundation, p.26.
2   James, W. (1899). *Talks to Teachers on Psychology: And to Students on Some of Life's Ideals.* New York: Henry Holt and Company, p.69.
3   Hattie, J., and Yates, G. (2013). *Visible Learning and the Science of How We Learn.* Abingdon: Routledge, p.219.
4   Berger, R. (2003). *An Ethic of Excellence.* Portsmouth, NH: Heinemann, p.8.
5   American Psychological Association, Coalition for Psychology in Schools and Education. (2015). *Top 20 Principles from Psychology for preK–12 Teaching and Learning,* p.13.
6   Dweck, C., Walton, G., and Cohen, G. (2011). *Academic Tenacity: Mindsets and Skills that Promote Long-Term Learning.* Seattle, WA: The Gates Foundation, p.26.
7   Hattie, J., and Yates, G. (2013). *Visible Learning and the Science of How We Learn.* Abingdon: Routledge, p.223.
8   ibid. p.222.
9   Berger, R. Cited in: Tough, P. (2016). *Helping Children Succeed: What Works and Why.* 1st ed. [PDF], p.113.

10 Hattie, J., and Yates, G. (2013). *Visible Learning and the Science of How We Learn.* Abingdon: Routledge, p.224.

11 Willingham, D. (2009). *Why Don't Students Like School?* San Francisco: Jossey-Bass, p.50.

12 Harvard University Center on the Developing Child. [Web page] *Executive Function & Self-Regulation.* Available at: http://developingchild.harvard.edu/science/key-concepts/executive-function

13 Willingham, D. (2011). Can Teachers Increase Students' Self-control? *American Educator*, Summer 2011, p.25.

14 Duckworth, A., Gendler, T., and Gross, J. (2016). Situational strategies for self-control. *Perspectives on Psychological Science*, 11(1), p.35.

15 ibid. p.50.

16 American Psychological Association, Coalition for Psychology in Schools and Education. (2015). *Top 20 Principles from Psychology for preK–12 Teaching and Learning*, pp.13–14.

17 Willingham, D. (2011). Can Teachers Increase Students' Self-control? *American Educator*, Summer 2011, p.26.

18 Dweck, C., Walton, G., and Cohen, G. (2011). *Academic Tenacity: Mindsets and Skills that Promote Long-Term Learning.* Seattle, WA: The Gates Foundation, p.21.

19 ibid. p.10.

20 American Psychological Association, Coalition for Psychology in Schools and Education. (2015). *Top 20 Principles from Psychology for preK–12 Teaching and Learning*, p.18.

21 Dweck, C., Walton, G., and Cohen, G. (2011). *Academic Tenacity: Mindsets and Skills that Promote Long-Term Learning.* Seattle, WA: The Gates Foundation, p.8.

22 ibid. p.31.

23 Wiliam, D. (2013). Assessment: The Bridge between Teaching and Learning. *Voices from the Middle*, 21(2), p.19.

24 Deans for Impact. (2015). *The Science of Learning.* Austin, TX: Deans for Impact, p.7.

25 Wiliam, D. (2015). Practical Ideas for Classroom Formative Assessment [Blog] *Dylan Wiliam Center Blog.* Available at: www.dylanwiliamcenter.com/practical-ideas-for-classroom-formative-assessment

26 Berger, R. (2003). *An Ethic of Excellence.* Portsmouth, NH: Heinemann, p.23.

27 Marzano, R. (2010). High Expectations for All. *Educational Leadership*, 68(1), pp.82–84.

28 Dweck, C., Walton, G., and Cohen, G. (2011). *Academic Tenacity: Mindsets and Skills that Promote Long-Term Learning.* Seattle, WA: The Gates Foundation, p.30.

29 Hattie, J. (2012). *Visible Learning for Teachers: Maximizing Impact on Learning.* Abingdon: Routledge, p.18.

30 James, W. (1899). *Talks to Teachers on Psychology: And to Students on Some of Life's Ideals.* New York: Henry Holt and Company, p.55.

31 Willingham, D. (2009). *Why Don't Students Like School?* San Francisco: Jossey-Bass, p.192.

32 Hattie, J. (2014). *Values-led and evidence-informed education – exploring what really makes a difference to learning.* [Keynote Lecture to Whole Education's 5th Annual

Conference]. London, 18 November 2014. Available at: https://visible-learning. org/2016/11/video-john-hatties-keynote-at-whole-education-conference

33 Duckworth, A. (2016). *Grit: The Power of Passion and Perseverance.* New York: Simon & Schuster, p.137.

34 Christodoulou, D. (2017). *Making Good Progress? The Future of Assessment for Learning.* Oxford: Oxford University Press, p.23.

35 Wiliam, D. (2011). *Embedded Formative Assessment.* Bloomington, IN: Solution Tree Press, p.145.

36 Hattie, J., and Yates, G. (2013). *Visible Learning and the Science of How We Learn.* Abingdon: Routledge, p.xvii.

37 Wiliam, D. Cited in Christodoulou, D. (2017). *Making Good Progress? The Future of Assessment for Learning.* Oxford: Oxford University Press, p.21.

38 Wiliam, D. (2011). *Embedded Formative Assessment.* Bloomington, IN: Solution Tree Press, p.152.

39 ibid. p.158.

40 American Psychological Association, Coalition for Psychology in Schools and Education. (2015). *Top 20 Principles from Psychology for preK–12 Teaching and Learning,* p.20.

41 Dweck, C., Walton, G., and Cohen, G. (2011). *Academic Tenacity: Mindsets and Skills that Promote Long-Term Learning.* Seattle, WA: The Gates Foundation, p.28.

8 Learning from other phases and subjects

Common ground

Something that intrigued me throughout my investigations was the similarity between the ways that primary and secondary teachers seemed to be approaching this area and, likewise, by the similarity in approach across different secondary subjects. I'm not sure what I was expecting, but I think I imagined that the approach to developing confidence, independence and resilience would be very different in Year 1 and Year 11, in French and in Maths. As it happened, I saw similar principles and techniques being applied in a wide range of different classrooms.

Saying that, I was struck by the way that different ages, subjects, school structures, and local contexts yielded different challenges, and required teachers to innovate to overcome them. The teachers I visited used a similar overall approach but, according to their situation, placed particular emphasis on certain outcomes and developed particular strengths as a consequence. Seeing this convinced me that there's great value in teachers who don't do the same thing, or teach in the same place, learning from one another.

For that reason, this guide contains practical examples from a mixture of locations, phases and subjects. It's also the reason why, as a general rule, examples aren't accompanied by information about the subject or year group they come from. Even if we don't mean to be swayed by them, these labels can be off-putting and imply that a certain idea or technique only has relevance to teachers in the same situation. If you're interested in the origin of a particular example, you can consult the list at the front of the book that outlines each teacher's phase, subject and location.

The Early Years

With the exception of one reception classroom, all of the examples in this book are drawn from Years 1 to 13. As such, I want to dwell for a moment on what teachers across the age range can learn from the way confidence, independence and resilience are developed in the Early Years.

Unique among the three phases of school education, in the Early Years a child's development is viewed and monitored holistically and there's an expectation that educators will focus explicitly on outcomes beyond the academic. For example, the guiding principles of the Early Years Statutory Framework (2014), include the statements that every child 'can be resilient, capable, confident and self-assured' and that 'children learn to be strong and independent through positive relationships'.[1] Confidence, independence and resilience are in the foreground of the aims and expectations for the under-fives, and practitioners are keenly aware of the multi-faceted, multi-layered nature of children's learning and development: that while pupils are working and playing they are simultaneously practising and learning other mindsets, skills and habits.

The way that Early Years practitioners assess children's learning and development is particularly instructive for our purposes. 'Practitioners watch, listen and interact as children engage in everyday activities, events and experiences, and demonstrate their specific knowledge, skills and understanding', says the Early years foundation stage profile: 2017 handbook.[2] Careful observation of pupil behaviour is viewed as a meaningful source of data, and ordinary teacher–child interactions are viewed as central to the assessment process. 'Much practitioner knowledge of what children know and can do will be gathered from day-to-day interactions', the handbook continues. It also stresses that 'practitioners should involve children fully in their own assessment by encouraging them to communicate about and review their own learning.' This description is similar to the observational evaluation proposed in this guide on p.44.

The other aspect of Early Years assessment that's particularly noteworthy is the simplicity and specificity of the statements that practitioners have on hand to help them assess intangible-sounding outcomes. For example, to assess the outcome 'Being willing to have a go', teachers are advised to watch for children showing the following behaviours:

- Finding an interest
- Initiating activities
- Seeking challenge
- Having a 'can do' attitude
- Being willing to take a risk in new experiences
- Developing the view that failures are opportunities to learn[3]

The Early Years Assessment Handbook also contains questions that teachers can ask themselves to consider how a child is progressing against a certain outcome. For example, in the 'Keeping on trying' outcome, teachers are asked:

- Does the child pursue a particular line of interest in an activity?
- Does the child demonstrate persistence in the face of difficulty or a challenge?
- Can the child re-focus and re-plan to overcome difficulties, setbacks and disappointments?
- Does the child know how to seek appropriate help in terms of materials, tools and other people?[4]

If you've already explored the rest of this guide, you'll see that the precision, tangibility and matter-of-factness of these assessment statements and questions is something that I've tried to emulate in the success criteria alongside the chart of pupil outcomes on p.6.

Perhaps the process of developing confidence, independence and resilience is more explicit in the Early Years simply because, when children are very young, it's so evident that they need to learn how to learn, and how to think positively about learning, as well as needing to learn academic content. Working with children who are new to the school environment demands a consideration of the mindsets, skills and habits that they need to focus, engage and achieve.

Notes

1 Department for Education (2014). *Statutory framework for the early years foundation stage*, p.6.
2 Standards and Testing Agency (2016). *Early years foundation stage profile: 2017 handbook*, p.11.
3 ibid.
4 ibid.

9 Exploring the evidence

What do we know now?

What follows is a brief summary of the current academic evidence, laying out what we know about the relative importance and malleability of the skills and mindsets on the outcomes chart on p.6. For ease of navigation, they are grouped here under one of our three overarching aims: confidence, independence and resilience. In reality, many of these mindsets and skills do not slot neatly into one place. 'Growth mindset', 'ownership' and 'intrinsic motivation', for example, cut across, and feed into, all three.

Confidence	Independence	Resilience
– Self-efficacy	– Self-control	– Persistence
– Growth mindset	– Intrinsic motivation	– Self-evaluation
– Positive attitude to, and openness about, mistakes and challenge	– Metacognitive strategies	– Ownership
– Risk taking		– Sustained effort
– Openness to, and engagement with, feedback		

The metacognitive strategies column on the outcomes chart is a distinct category: practical techniques you can teach pupils that allow them to help themselves and that underpin the other mindsets and habits on the flowchart. They are grouped together here under 'independence' and dealt with collectively.

One challenge in summarising this evidence is matching the outcomes in this guide with the terms used in academic papers; terminology can vary from paper to paper and, often, the concepts studied by academics are fairly broad, encompassing more than one of the outcomes on our flowchart. I've made a note where there's mismatching terminology and made it clear when an academic concept relates to more than one of the outcomes in this guide.

Confidence

Self-efficacy

> #### Potential impact
>
> The way that children think about themselves and their ability is enormously important in the classroom: if positive, it can underpin a range of other positive outcomes; if negative, it can be a terrible barrier to motivation, effort and persistence. Dweck, Walton and Cohen stress the powerful impact that high self-efficacy can have on learning:
>
> > Research shows that students' belief in their ability to learn and perform well in school – their *self-efficacy* – can predict their level of academic performance above and beyond their measured level of ability and prior performance.[1]
>
> Likewise the EEF literature review states that '[c]hildren's perception of their ability, their expectations of future success, and the extent to which they value an activity influence their motivation and persistence leading to improved academic outcomes, especially for low-attaining pupils.'[2]
>
> #### Malleability
>
> This area is considered to be malleable. '[S]elf-concept of ability is malleable for school-age populations', according to the EEF's literature review. Likewise, the review suggests that 'self-efficacy for a particular task is malleable and that improved self-efficacy is associated with greater persistence, interest, and performance.'[3]

Self-efficacy, in the EEF's definition, 'measures an individual's expectations about whether or not they can successfully perform a specific task at a later point in time.'[4] To use John Hattie and Gregory Yates's definition, 'your efficacy is confidence for succeeding on the very task you can see there in front of you.' It involves 'an actual judgement, made in real time' about whether you can do something.[5] As such, self-efficacy beliefs are hugely important in the classroom and determine the likelihood of a pupil feeling motivated, making an effort, taking risks and persisting through challenge. The EEF review describes high self-efficacy as 'an essential precursor to enhancing both cognitive and non-cognitive skills' and makes the point that 'young people may be more willing to persist when they believe they are going to succeed'.[6] This may sound basic, even self-evident, but it's a critical link in the chain and it's essential to ensure that it's in place.

There's a basic logic to levels of self-efficacy. If you tend to fail at something, it will be low. If you tend to do well at something, it will be much higher. As Professor Rob Coe has pointed out, 'the poor motivation of low attainers is a logical response to repeated failure. Start getting them to succeed and their motivation and confidence should increase.'[7] The principal mechanism for increasing self-efficacy beliefs, therefore, is to support pupils to experience success. As Hattie and Yates write, '[to] feel confident about the next task, you must be able to activate knowledge about similar tasks you were successful on in the past.'[8] Teachers need to provide pupils with memories of past success to inspire future effort and persistence. The EEF review puts it like this:

> [T]here is likely to be a reciprocal relationship between self-efficacy and academic performance: strong performance validates self-efficacy, increases motivation, and reinforces effort and persistence toward achievement.[9]

A key point that Hattie and Yates make is that low self-efficacy 'can often have a basis in skills deficits or genuine knowledge gaps'.[10] Where this is the case, teachers need to concentrate on urgently filling those gaps, while still seeking to build self-efficacy by providing pupils with the opportunity to succeed at appropriately challenging work.

The problem with self-esteem

Self-esteem, another dimension of confidence and self-perception, is quite consciously absent from our chart of outcomes. Although low self-esteem can be damaging in the classroom, it needs careful handling within this process. Self-esteem is not something to pursue head-on, but rather something that should be seen as a welcome side-effect of effort and achievement.

Martin Seligman describes the risks of prioritising self-esteem in the classroom:

> Failure and feeling bad are necessary building blocks for ultimate success and feeling good. [. . .] Children need to fail. They need to feel sad, anxious and angry. [. . .] When they encounter obstacles, if we leap in to bolster self-esteem [. . .] to soften the blows and to distract them with congratulatory ebullience, we make it harder for them to achieve mastery.[11]

Pupils need to feel safe and supported, but that doesn't mean that they shouldn't also feel uncomfortable and frustrated at times. Hattie and Yates reinforce Seligman's point, writing that 'increases in general esteem follow on from success in school, but do not predict such success.'[12]

Growth mindset

This section also covers the following outcomes:

- *Positive attitude to, and openness about, mistakes and challenge*
- *Risk taking*
- *Openness to, and engagement with, feedback*

Potential impact

'When individuals believe that they can increase their ability through their own efforts, they are more motivated, put forth sustained effort and persistence, and use strategies to accomplish their goals,' remarks the EEF review,[13] describing the power of what Carol Dweck calls a 'growth mindset'. The value of approaching learning with a growth mindset is increasingly acknowledged and championed. 'Students who believe that intelligence can be improved with hard work', writes Daniel Willingham, 'get higher grades than students who believe that intelligence is an immutable trait.'[14] Angela Duckworth also confirms its importance: 'If you have a growth mindset, you're more likely to do well in school, enjoy better emotional and physical health, and have stronger, more positive social relationships with other people.'[15]

Malleability

There is evidence that pupils can develop a growth mindset. However, as Dweck points out, it's not quite as simple as 'having' or 'not having' a growth mindset. '[W]e're all a mixture of fixed and growth mindsets', she writes, and '[. . .] probably always will be'.[16] For more on this point, see p.68.

Carol Dweck's research demonstrates that pupils who believe they can develop their intelligence try harder and do better than those who believe that they have a fixed level of intelligence. Those whose mindset is more fixed, Dweck writes, often 'mobilise their resources, not for learning, but to protect their egos. And one of the main ways they do this [. . .] is by not trying.'[17] The tragedy here is that some pupils invest a lot of effort to avoid risking short term failure, rather than taking the risks that lead to learning and long term success. Describing the differing perspectives on effort, mistakes and failure that emerge according to whether you have a fixed or growth mindset, Dweck writes:

> When you enter a mindset, you enter a new world. [. . .] In one world, failure is about having a setback. Getting a bad grade. Losing a tournament. Getting fired. Getting rejected. It means you're not smart or talented. In the other world, failure is about not growing. Not reaching for the things you value. It means you're not fulfilling your potential. In one world, effort is a bad thing. It, like failure, means you're not smart or talented. If you were, you wouldn't need effort. In the other world, effort is what makes you smart or talented.[18]

The potential advantages of a growth mindset are manifold: optimism, improved self-perception, a willingness to seek help, a belief in the power of practice, among other things. This mindset unlocks many other beliefs and actions.

Independence

Self-control

Potential Impact

The EEF review defines self-control as 'the ability to resist short-term impulses in order to prioritise longer-term goals.'[19] It's powerful: according to research by the Duckworth Lab it 'predicts report card grades (and changes in report card grades over time) better than does measured intelligence.'[20]

Malleability

Self-control is a somewhat knotty quality. Although it's considered a personality trait, people can improve this capacity through practice, and develop habits and strategies that enable them to act in a more self-controlled fashion.

Self-control seems to be both a trait that can be developed over time and a set of habits and strategies that can be deployed at any time. Essentially, it is to do with resisting temptations in favour of less immediately appealing, but ultimately more important, aims. Daniel Willingham (using the term 'self-regulation') refers to it as 'the ability to inhibit the automatic response and to do something else [. . .] the ability to control one's emotions, to control attention and other cognitive processes, and to plan and control behavior. This capacity', he writes, 'turns out to have enormous consequences for academic and social success.'[21]

The EEF review makes the following points about the extent to which self-control can be changed:

- It seems 'that individuals can strengthen their ability to control their feelings, desires, and motivations through practice or exercise'.
- '[S]elf-control may be considered a personality trait' but it can be simulated by using strategies for delaying gratification.
- 'Circumstances may make it easier or more difficult to control one's impulses'.[22]

Intrinsic motivation

Potential impact

The EEF review contains the tantalising statement that 'children's expectations for success in combination with valuing the task are the strongest predictors of subsequent performance'.[23] 'Expectations of success' is covered by self-efficacy above. 'Valuing the task' – motivation, in other words – is the other crucial component. The major question here is whether pupils are motivated by internal or external factors; although extrinsic motivation can play an important role in the classroom, intrinsic motivation is ultimately a far more powerful driver of pupil progress. According to the EEF review, 'contexts which highlight intrinsic versus extrinsic-related goals encourage greater motivation, more persistence, and higher achievement for students of all ages.'[24]

Malleability

The nature of pupils' motivations is considered to be malleable.

There are moments when using extrinsic factors to motivate pupils in the classroom is entirely appropriate. However, when it comes to developing their confidence, independence and resilience, there is enormous value in working on pupils' intrinsic motivations. As well as being the spark that, together with self-efficacy, prompts effort, intrinsic motivation can ensure that pupils are doing what they're doing willingly and in relation to their own aims, rather than because they feel compelled to. As such, the EEF review states, intrinsic motivation is also 'positively related to psychological well-being and positive adjustment.'[25]

The nature of our motivations is thought to be influenced by the context in which we find ourselves, suggesting that 'teachers can help shape students' intrinsic motivation for learning through their teaching methods and classroom environment.'[26] One way that this can happen, according to the EEF review, is 'as a result of autonomous, self-determined decisions that give individuals a sense of control and power.'[27] In other words, providing pupils with opportunities to make choices, take control of their learning and consider how the classroom connects to their own aims and interests can help to foster intrinsic motivation. Likewise, Deci and Ryan write that: 'Classroom contexts where students experience autonomy, competence, and relatedness [social belonging] tend not only to foster more intrinsic motivation, but also more willing engagement in less interesting academic activities.'[28]

Metacognitive strategies

This section covers the following outcomes:

– *Strategies for deflecting distractions*
– *Strategies for working effectively with peers*

- *Strategies for dealing with and learning from mistakes*
- *Skill in giving, receiving and acting on feedback*
- *Strategies for approaching independent work and overcoming challenges*
- *Skill in selecting work at an appropriately challenging level*
- *Skill in self-assessment and goal setting*
- *Skill in managing time and resources*
- *Strategies to make practice effective*

Potential impact

Metacognitive strategies are techniques that pupils can draw on to support themselves. Pupils decide independently when and how to use them. The EEF gives the following examples, 'setting goals, planning and problem-solving, being aware of one's strengths and weakness, monitoring one's progress and understanding', and states that metacognitive strategies have 'been shown to have medium to large effects on a number of academic outcomes.'[29]

Malleability

Metacognitive strategies 'are malleable and can be taught or otherwise developed in students from primary school to university and across a wide range of academic subjects', according to the EEF.[30]

This category can be thought of as a kind of mental toolbox: the roster of strategies that pupils have at their disposal at any given moment. They buttress the other outcomes on our flowchart: intrinsic motivation and persistence become rather empty qualities if they aren't underpinned by strategies that support pupils to navigate challenges and complete their work.

In the EEF review's definition, using metacognitive strategies is an attempt 'to influence one's own learning behaviours and processes'. This involves 'selecting, monitoring, and planning strategies that are most conducive to learning'. The significant point here is not simply possessing important skills, but 'knowing when and why to use' them.[31]

Metacognitive strategies can look quite different across the age range. '[Y]ounger children are more likely to use overt strategies such as talking aloud during problem-solving [...],' according to the EEF review, 'while older children are more likely to use complex strategies such as evaluating their own style of learning and assessing what they know and what they do not know (i.e., self-appraisal).' However, the principle – having strategies at your fingertips and selecting between them – is identical regardless of age.

Resilience

Persistence

Potential impact

'It is virtually impossible to become proficient at a mental task without extended practice', writes Daniel Willingham.[32] As such, persistence – the willingness to stick at challenging tasks and conduct hard, sometimes repetitive, practice – is an extremely significant outcome for pupils.

Malleability

Persistence hinges on a range of factors and can definitely be improved.

Persistence, sticking at something even if it's challenging, is a crucial, everyday quality – but can be rather fragile to begin with. It's contingent on pupils' self-efficacy and motivations, and needs to be underpinned by metacognitive strategies that enable pupils to solve problems, seek help where necessary and respond to feedback. Persistence is essential in order for pupils to grapple with challenging work and engage in the practice that will embed key knowledge and skills.

'There is a wealth of research showing that students' persistence at tasks changes over time and in different situations,' states the EEF review, 'including studies [...] showing that high self-efficacy, a mastery goal orientation [growth mindset], and intrinsic motivation relate to increased persistence at tasks.'[33] The University of Chicago review also notes that 'numerous instructional practices [...] have been shown to improve students' perseverance [...] by changing students' mindsets.'[34]

Ownership, self-evaluation and sustained effort

The academic construct that encompasses these three outcomes is 'grit', Angela Duckworth's term for the quality that leads a person to pursue a challenging long-term goal over a sustained period.

Potential Impact

Once pupils believe they can do something and feel motivated to make an effort, they need the resilience to see it through – both persistence in the moment and the drive to sustain effort over a longer period. Angela Duckworth has coined the term 'grit' to describe this latter quality: a kind of super-charged persistence that entails a willingness to weather challenge over an extended period in pursuit of a significant long term goal. 'Because high levels of achievement require sustained effort on difficult tasks, grit will be an important predictor of remaining in and succeeding in school', write Dweck, Walton and Cohen. 'Although grit is unrelated to IQ, it predicts educational attainment.'[35]

Malleability

Grit tends to be thought of as a personality trait, rather than a mutable skill or mindset. Duckworth's research suggests that levels of grittiness can change as people's mindsets change and as people gain different life experiences.

Grit is a multi-faceted construct and, as such, doesn't appear on our chart as a standalone outcome. However research into grit provides us with a useful evidence base for considering the longerterm, self-directed aspect of resilience, represented in this guide by the trio of **ownership, self-evaluation** and **sustained effort**. Angela Duckworth describes grit as follows:

> Grit entails working strenuously towards challenges, maintaining effort and interest over years despite failure, adversity, and plateaus in progress. [...] Whereas disappointment or boredom signals to others that it is time to change trajectory and cut losses, the gritty individual stays the course.[36]

Grit has become something of an educational buzzword and is sometimes just used to mean 'dogged perseverance'. However, as Duckworth's Character Lab puts it: 'Grit is much more than just encouraging kids to "try harder" or not give up – it's also about helping kids find their passion.'[37] In this way, it relates to the idea of 'ownership' on our chart and it's in line with some of the points about motivation above – being able to connect day-to-day work in the classroom with significant personal aims in the longer term. The EEF states that grit should be considered more of a 'stable personality trait' than a malleable skill.[38] Duckworth puts it this way:

> The language we use to describe grit and self-control – words like "character" or "personality trait"– may connote some immutability. However, it is now well-established that traits change across the life course [...]. So, while there is enough stability to traits to sensibly describe one individual as grittier than another, it is also true that children and adults change their habitual patterns of interacting with the world as they accumulate additional life experience.[39]

That is to say, we may be more or less gritty at a given moment, but this is a quality that can be nurtured over time, and we can also learn ways of thinking and acting that enable us to act in more gritty ways.

Grit has attracted a great deal of attention in recent debates about character and non-cognitive skills, perhaps more than any other single outcome. As such, it may appear curious that it doesn't feature more prominently in this guide. The reason for this is partly that grit is a construct that encapsulates a range of mindsets and habits. But another, perhaps more important reason, is the fact that, in Duckworth's words, grit is 'about holding the same top-level goal for a very long time', perhaps many years.[40] While there's much in this guide about the value of setting ambitious goals and discussing the future in the classroom, it didn't feel appropriate to suggest that all pupils, regardless of age and circumstances, should settle upon one 'top-level goal' that they pursue single-mindedly for years.

Combinations

One overall point that emerges powerfully from the academic research into this area is that it's essential to think about these outcomes holistically. These skills and mindsets acquire meaning and power from one another; the teacher's role is to choreograph their development. The EEF literature review puts it like this:

> When developed in combination, skills such as self-efficacy, motivation, and metacognitive strategies appear to be influential in improving academic learning and success in children and young people.[41]

However, as the University of Chicago review states, 'it is unclear how all the different types of noncognitive factors interact to shape academic performance or what their implications are for educational practice.'[42] In the chart on p.6, to support you to think about how to develop these mindsets, skills and habits in combination, outcomes are sequenced across three phases and arrows suggest the relationships between them. This is a best guess based on existing research, which can be refined as further evidence emerges.

Notes

1 Dweck, C., Walton, G., and Cohen, G. (2011). *Academic Tenacity: Mindsets and Skills that Promote Long-Term Learning.* Seattle, WA: The Gates Foundation, p.5.
2 Gutman, L. and Schoon, I. (2013). *The Impact of Non-Cognitive Skills on Outcomes for Young People.* London: Institute of Education, Education Endowment Foundation, Cabinet Office, p.2.
3 ibid. p.11.
4 ibid. p.10.
5 Hattie, J. and Yates, G. (2013). *Visible Learning and the Science of How We Learn.* Abingdon: Routledge, p.219.
6 Gutman, L. and Schoon, I. (2013). *The Impact of Non-Cognitive Skills on Outcomes for Young People.* London: Institute of Education, Education Endowment Foundation, Cabinet Office, p.11.
7 Coe, R., Aloisi, C., Higgins, S., and Major, L. (2014) *What Makes Great Teaching? Review of the Underpinning Research.* London: Sutton Trust, p.23.
8 Hattie, J. and Yates, G. (2013). *Visible Learning and the Science of How We Learn.* Abingdon: Routledge, p.221.
9 See note 6.
10 Hattie, J. and Yates, G. (2013). *Visible Learning and the Science of How We Learn.* Abingdon: Routledge, p.223.
11 Seligman, M. (2007). *The Optimistic Child.* New York: Houghton Mifflin Company, pp.44–45.
12 Hattie, J. and Yates, G. (2013). *Visible Learning and the Science of How We Learn.* Abingdon: Routledge, p.223.
13 Gutman, L. and Schoon, I. (2013). *The Impact of Non-Cognitive Skills on Outcomes for Young People.* London: Institute of Education, Education Endowment Foundation, Cabinet Office, p.12.
14 Willingham, D. (2009). *Why Don't Students Like School?* San Francisco: Jossey-Bass, p.180.
15 Duckworth, A. (2016). *Grit: The Power of Passion and Perseverance.* New York: Simon & Schuster, p.181.
16 Dweck, C. (2015). Carol Dweck Revisits the 'Growth Mindset' [Online]. Education Week. Available at: www.edweek.org/ew/articles/2015/09/23/carol-dweck-revisits-the-growth-mindset.html
17 Dweck, C. (2006). *Mindset: The New Psychology of Success.* New York: Ballantine Books, p.58.
18 ibid. p.15.

19 Gutman, L. and Schoon, I. (2013). *The Impact of Non-Cognitive Skills on Outcomes for Young People*. London: Institute of Education, Education Endowment Foundation, Cabinet Office, p.20.

20 Duckworth, A. (2015). Research Statement [Online]. The Duckworth Lab. Available at: www.authentichappiness.sas.upenn.edu/learn/grit

21 Willingham, D. (2011). Can Teachers Increase Students' Self-control? *American Educator*, Summer 2011, p.22.

22 Gutman, L. and Schoon, I. (2013). *The Impact of Non-Cognitive Skills on Outcomes for Young People*. London: Institute of Education, Education Endowment Foundation, Cabinet Office, p.21.

23 ibid. p.16.

24 ibid. p.15.

25 ibid. p.14.

26 ibid. p.15.

27 ibid. p.14.

28 Ryan, R. and Deci, E. (2013). Toward a Social Psychology of Assimilation: Self-Determination Theory in Cognitive Development and Education. In: B. Sokol, F. Grouzet and U. Müller, eds., *Self Regulation and Autonomy: Social and Developmental Dimensions of Human Conduct*, 1st ed. Cambridge, MA: Cambridge University Press, p.199.

29 Gutman, L. and Schoon, I. (2013). *The Impact of Non-Cognitive Skills on Outcomes for Young People*. London: Institute of Education, Education Endowment Foundation, Cabinet Office, p.23.

30 ibid.

31 ibid. p.22.

32 Willingham, D. (2009). *Why Don't Students Like School?* San Francisco: Jossey-Bass, p.107.

33 Gutman, L. and Schoon, I. (2013). *The Impact of Non-Cognitive Skills on Outcomes for Young People*. London: Institute of Education, Education Endowment Foundation, Cabinet Office, p.19.

34 Farrington, C.A., Roderick, M., Allensworth, E., Nagaoka, J., Keyes, T.S., Johnson, D.W., and Beechum, N.O. (2012). *Teaching Adolescents to Become Learners. The Role of Non-Cognitive Factors in Shaping School Performance: A Critical Literature Review*. Chicago: University of Chicago Consortium on Chicago School Research, p.79.

35 Dweck, C., Walton, G., and Cohen, G. (2011). *Academic Tenacity: Mindsets and Skills that Promote Long-Term Learning*. Seattle, WA: The Gates Foundation, p.13.

36 Duckworth, A., Peterson, C., Matthews, D., and Kelly, R. (2007). Grit: Perseverance and Passion for Long-Term Goals. *Journal of Personality and Social Psychology*, 92(6), p.1088.

37 Character Lab. Grit. [Webpage]. Available at: https://characterlab.org/tools/grit

38 See note 2.

39 Duckworth, A. (2015). Research Statement [Online]. *The Duckworth Lab*. Accessed May 2015. Available at: https://sites.sas.upenn.edu/duckworth/pages/research-statement

40 Duckworth, A. (2016). *Grit: The Power of Passion and Perseverance*. New York: Simon & Schuster, p.64.

41 Gutman, L. and Schoon, I. (2013). *The Impact of Non-Cognitive Skills on Outcomes for Young People*. London: Institute of Education, Education Endowment Foundation, Cabinet Office, p.43.

42 Farrington, C.A., Roderick, M., Allensworth, E., Nagaoka, J., Keyes, T.S., Johnson, D.W., and Beechum, N.O. (2012). *Teaching Adolescents to Become Learners. The Role of Non-Cognitive Factors in Shaping School Performance: A Critical Literature Review*. Chicago: University of Chicago Consortium on Chicago School Research, p.6.

CONCLUSION

Across the pond

There has been a lot of talk in recent years about the role of schools in developing character. Often when the question arises, the spotlight swings over the Atlantic to the KIPP chain of Charter Schools in the United States. For some years now KIPP schools have made a concerted and well-publicised effort to instil character in their pupils and, as such, they've become the go-to example for educators interested in this area.

KIPP (the 'Knowledge is Power Program') was founded in 1994 by two Teach For America alumni, and the story behind their decision to focus on character is a compelling one. In their early days, KIPP opened schools in the poorest neighbourhoods and focused relentlessly on supporting pupils to get academic results that would transport them to university and, they hoped, a lifetime of expanded opportunities. KIPP Academy Middle School in the Bronx, the second KIPP school to open, came to national attention in 1999 when their first cohort achieved the fifth highest results in New York in their 8th-grade tests. The success story continued and the majority of that class made it to university. Once there, however, it became clear that all was not well: many of those headline-grabbing pupils struggled and dropped out.

This distressing realisation led KIPP to reappraise how well their highly structured, supportive school context was preparing pupils to face, and persevere with, academic and personal challenges independently. Their conclusion was that they needed to focus more intensively on the personal qualities that would enable pupils to persevere through university, and they worked with the psychologists Martin Seligman, Chris Peterson and Angela Duckworth to formulate a list. Once that list of qualities had been agreed, the issue of how to develop them remained. Looking back in 2015, KIPP co-founder Dave Levin recalled the big question on his mind: 'We all agree these things are important, so how exactly do you nurture them? How exactly do you teach them?'[1] Today KIPP teachers follow a well-established model, which has features in common with the approach outlined in this guide: modelling key mindsets and skills; explicitly talking about them in class; planning learning experiences that require them; praising pupils when they demonstrate them; and tracking and discussing progress in this area. Having made this and other changes the university completion rates of KIPP pupils are on the rise: in 2011 33% of their pupils graduated from a four-year university degree; in 2015 that figure was 44% (about five times higher than the US average for pupils from low-income backgrounds, 9%, and above the overall US average, 34%. KIPP's objective is 75%).[2]

KIPP wouldn't claim that they've perfected their approach to character; what's most inspiring in their example is the fact that, having identified an issue for their pupils, they went looking for solutions, even when there wasn't solid evidence of what would be effective. In the process, they pioneered practices that can be studied and improved, inspired others to do likewise, and catalysed a lively, productive debate.

Closer to home

KIPP's story is thought-provoking and I'm glad to air it here, but their approach to character is embedded into such a distinctive, structured school environment that it's not necessarily an easy example for an individual teacher to learn from. My experience visiting classrooms convinced me that we can and should look for examples of innovation closer to home too, and learn from teachers working in a wide variety of contexts.

Yet current research and debate in the UK tends to overlook what happens in the classroom day-to-day, focusing instead on the value of additional courses and interventions: programmes for developing character and non-cognitive skills through, among other things, sport, music, mentoring, philosophy, scouting, volunteering and public speaking. I have no wish to discourage the promotion of additional courses, coaching, camps and clubs for young people – they're fun and they can have all manner of benefits. However, I worry that this focus on extra-curricular activities stems from a wariness about whether character can be developed in the classroom at all, and a fear of burdening teachers with extra responsibilities.

It's often said that character and non-cognitive skills aren't 'teachable'. This idea appears prominently in Paul Tough's recent book *Helping Children Succeed*, which claims that rather than 'trying to "teach" skills like grit and self-control, we should focus instead on creating the kinds of environments, both at home and at school, in which those qualities are most likely to flourish.'[3] But Tough's point isn't that teachers can't make a difference, it's that they should come at these mindsets and skills side-on, developing them through their classroom environment, rather than trying to teach them in standalone lessons.

We neglect the classroom at our peril. Pupils spend many more hours there than they can spend at clubs or residential courses, and teachers are uniquely well placed to get to know pupils and work on these outcomes over an extended period. What's more, the challenges of academic learning provide a perfect foil for the development of other mindsets, skills and habits. It's critical that all teachers know that they *can* influence their pupils' confidence, independence and resilience, and believe that doing so is a core part of their role.

'When educators neither prioritize these skills and mindsets nor integrate them with academic development, students are left without tools for engagement or a language for learning', writes Brooke Stafford-Brizard. 'They become dependent on adult-driven procedures and routines rather than their own skills and motivation.'[4] As this comment makes clear, prioritising these outcomes is not just about helping young people to progress academically – something that could equally be achieved by hand-holding and spoon-feeding – it's about respecting and trusting young people enough to equip them with the skills and mindsets to try, persist and succeed under their own steam, to hand them ownership of their learning, and to enable them to connect the things they do at school to their broader hopes and interests.

Summary and recommendations

In summary, although there's widespread agreement that this area is important, there's ongoing debate around which outcomes matter most, how to address them, and in what context. More research is required, but in the meantime we can point to teachers who are successfully developing their pupils' confidence, independence and resilience, and learn and share lessons from their classrooms.

In this guide, I've sought to do just that, mapping out key outcomes and proposing a model to support you to address them within and through academic learning. Although it requires planning, consistent application, and ongoing evaluation, there's no wizardry to this approach. If anything, the biggest step is the first: believing that you can have an impact on these outcomes through your teaching at all. Once you do, it's a question of crafting an environment in which pupils are constantly practising the mindsets, skills and habits that they need to develop.

I've focused throughout this book on the classroom rather than the school level. This is to ensure that this guide is meaningful for any teacher in any school. There are, of course, considerable benefits to taking a unified approach to developing confidence, independence and resilience. The model and strategies outlined in this guide could equally be applied at a whole-school level, with all teachers focusing on an agreed set of mindsets, skills and habits in consistent ways so that what pupils experience in one classroom is reinforced in all the others, and what they learn one year is consolidated in the years that follow.

It's my belief that, of the many things that schools can do to address the achievement gap between rich and poor, the potential for impact here is particularly high, and the need for additional time and resources refreshingly low. My concluding recommendations for schools and teachers, therefore, are:

- To embrace and spread the idea that teachers can have a major influence on pupils' confidence, independence and resilience within and through academic learning.
- To develop key mindsets, skills and habits in the classroom deliberately and systematically.
- To investigate this area further at ground level: testing ideas, developing new strategies and sharing what you learn.

If, as the then Education Secretary Nicky Morgan said in 2014, the UK wants to become a 'global leader in teaching character and resilience'[5], my recommendations for the broader education community are:

- To maintain the momentum around this subject, continuing to debate these issues and share ideas and research.
- To be bold in discarding distracting terminology such as 'character' and 'non-cognitive skills' and name specific outcomes instead.
- To further investigate the mindsets and skills that have the greatest influence on pupil learning, how they develop, and how to evaluate them.
- To empower teachers with the belief that they can have an impact on their pupils' confidence, independence and resilience, and train and encourage them to do so.

Believing you can't succeed; avoiding effort; giving up... the vicious cycle described by the teachers in this guide undermines and dilutes so much else that is done to support pupils. Remove this barrier, by fostering confidence, independence and resilience, and you have a tremendous impact not only on young people's academic results, but also on their happiness, hopefulness, sense of agency, and on the opportunities they have in life.

I hope this guide enables you to support your pupils in this area, helps you to develop and share ideas of your own, and helps to take this debate forward.

Notes

1 Levin, D. (2015). Interviewed in: Character Lessons. [Radio programme] *The Educators*. BBC Radio 4. Available at: www.bbc.co.uk/programmes/b06ptw79
2 KIPP online data. Available at: www.kipp.org/results/national
3 Blurb for *Helping Children Succeed* by P. Tough (2016). Available at: http://paultough.com/helping/.
4 Stafford-Brizard, B. (2016). *Building Blocks for Learning: A Framework for Comprehensive Student Development*. Turnaround for Children, p.4.
5 Morgan, N. (2014). England to become a global leader of teaching character. [Press Release] Department for Education, 16 December 2014. Available at: www.gov.uk/government/news/england-to-become-a-global-leader-of-teaching-character

FURTHER READING

The following books and papers particularly informed and inspired this guide and are a good starting point for those looking to explore this area further.

Books

William James: *Talks to Teachers on Psychology: And to Students on Some of Life's Ideals* (1899).
Carol Dweck: *Mindset: The New Psychology of Success* (2006).
Daniel Willingham: *Why Don't Students Like School?* (2009).
Dylan Wiliam: *Embedded Formative Assessment* (2011).
John Hattie and Greg Yates: *Visible Learning and the Science of How We Learn* (2013).
Doug Lemov: *Teach Like a Champion 2.0* (2015).
Angela Duckworth: *Grit: The Power of Passion and Perseverance* (2016).
Paul Tough: *Helping Children Succeed: What works and Why* (2016).

Papers

Duckworth, A., Peterson, C., Matthews, D., and Kelly, R. (2007). Grit: Perseverance and Passion for Long-Term Goals. *Journal of Personality and Social Psychology*, 92(6), p.1088.
Center on the Developing Child at Harvard University (2011). *Building the Brain's "Air Traffic Control" System: How Early Experiences Shape the Development of Executive Function: Working Paper No. 11*.
Dweck, C., Walton, G., and Cohen, G. (2011). *Academic Tenacity: Mindsets and Skills that Promote Long-Term Learning*. Seattle, WA: The Gates Foundation.
Willingham, D. (2011). Can Teachers Increase Students' Self-control? *American Educator*, Summer 2011.
Farrington, C.A., Roderick, M., Allensworth, E., Nagaoka, J., Keyes, T.S., Johnson, D.W., and Beechum, N.O. (2012). *Teaching Adolescents to Become Learners. The Role of Noncognitive Factors in Shaping School Performance: A Critical Literature Review*. Chicago: University of Chicago Consortium on Chicago School Research.

Gutman, L., and Schoon, I. (2013). *The Impact of Non-cognitive Skills on Outcomes for Young People*. London: Institute of Education, Education Endowment Foundation, Cabinet Office.

Paterson, C., Tyler, C., and Lexmond, J. (2014). *Character and Resilience Manifesto*. London: The All-Party Parliamentary Group on Social Mobility, Centre Forum, Character Counts.

Reeves, R., Venator, J., and Howard, K. (2014). *The Character Factor: Measures and Impact of Drive and Prudence*. The Brookings Institution.

Stafford-Brizard, B. (2016). *Building Blocks for Learning: A Framework for Comprehensive Student Development*. Turnaround for Children.

INDEX

ACKNOWLEDGEMENTS

First of all, enormous thanks to the many teachers and students who welcomed the Teach First Knowledge Development team into their lessons, and to their schools for granting us the permission to visit. It's rarely convenient to have extra people cluttering corridors, crowding classrooms and conducting interviews in staffrooms and store cupboards. Our research simply wouldn't have been possible without the openness and generosity we experienced and I can't express my gratitude strongly enough. Tragically, Stephen Hughes, a superb primary teacher I visited in the North East, has since died from Giant Cell Myocarditis, and is remembered through the work of the Stephen Hughes Foundation. He was a hugely dynamic and inspiring individual, adored by his pupils, and I feel honoured to have met him and seen him teach.

Several people were particularly instrumental as I developed this guide. Many thanks indeed to Harry Fletcher-Wood, Sam Freedman, Jessica Heal, Alice Luetchford, Catherine Meenan and Rachel Parkin. Huge thanks also to Henry Eliot, Nick Hassey, Joe Kirby, Phil McComish, Belinda Sherlock and Barbara Trevitt for reading a draft of the book and providing invaluable feedback. Thanks to Isabel Greenberg for her delightful cover illustration.

Many others provided support, insight and encouragement during the creation of this guide. My thanks to Chris Brolly, Becky Donaldson, Alice Dunn, James Emanuel, Siobhan Haire, Nick Haisman-Smith, Hanna McCloskey, Andreas Michaels, Reuben Moore, Dan Morrison, Nicole Quenault, Vidhu Sood-Nicholls, Amanda Timberg and Patrick Walsh. Thanks also to all past and present members of the marvellous Research, Evaluation and Impact department and to all of my former colleagues at Teach First.

It's been a pleasure working with the team at Routledge. My thanks in particular to Clare Ashworth for being such a positive and insightful editor.

Thanks also to Alice Gray, Annamarie Kino-Wylam and Sarah Richardson, and to Colin Read and the team at Sunrise Setting.

Massive love and thanks, as ever, to my parents and sister, Stephen, Julie and Jennifer Lloyd. And, above all, thanks to my magnificent wife Lydia and my new daughter Florence. It would be a stretch to say that Florence's birth made the writing of this book easier, but her arrival transformed the final period of drafting and grafting into the best of times.